Keep Eating
Mary

[signature]

Whos ~
Ana, ~
Having you & Mary as
part of The Goodfark family
means so much to s.
Happy Holidays
Love SHo
Love DEE♥

KOREAN HOME COOKING

RAYON

Your Rap game is on point!
Always laugh your way thru
life … Love you forever my
friend ♥ Heather

CLASSIC AND MODERN RECIPES

KOREAN
HOME
COOKING

SOHUI KIM WITH RACHEL WHARTON

ABRAMS, NEW YORK

Despite the obligatory no smiling policy for
Koreans taking pictures in the seventies, these
photos show what was actually a very fun and festive
sixtieth birthday party for my grandmother. (She's
in the yellow *hanbok*, the traditional Korean dress.
Next to her, looking smashing in a ruffled orange
and brown dress, is me!) My mother and grandmother
spent days cooking for the party, and my father
(the cool dude in sunglasses) hosted the party at
our house in Seoul on a beautiful day in May.

INTRODUCTION

My first job in my grandmother's kitchen was to plate the *banchan* for the family's evening dinner. Some nights, it would only be two or three little dishes to go with fluffy steamed rice and *doenjang jjigae*, a soothing bowl of silky potatoes, soft tofu, and sweet squash stewed with the nutty Korean soybean paste. If we were having guests over or celebrating a birthday, I helped bring out the large black lacquered dinner table and filled it with homemade goodies: marinated steamed eggplant from the garden; soy-pickled perilla leaves I helped to harvest the week prior; pan-fried eggs rolled with diced vegetables; sun-dried radishes from last year's harvest spiked with vinegar and fiery pepper flakes; and dried squid doused with honey and the chile paste called *gochujang*.

There might have also been *japchae*, glossy, slinky sweet potato starch noodles tossed with half a dozen vegetables; a whole fresh fish salted overnight and simply broiled; steamed egg custard with pollack roe; kimchi, usually both napa cabbage and cubed moo radish; crunchy squares of roasted seaweed; and *ganjang gaejang*, soy-marinated raw female crab filled with roe, claws crushed to soak up the brine. Finally, the thinly sliced, sweet soy-marinated and pan-seared *bulgogi* would hit the table.

My favorites were the egg custard, the marinated eggplant, and the seaweed, but especially the bulgogi. I would covet the sauce rather than the beef itself, tilting the bowl so I could scoop it out and pour it over my rice with a little kimchi.

I look back now and know how amazing it was to have experienced this traditional Korean way of eating and cooking in my native country, if only as a small child. I moved to the United States when I was ten, and my family quickly embraced American culinary habits. We still ate Korean food, but we got pizza delivered, too. (Though my dad would put kimchi on it.)

Flash forward thirty-five years later: I'm a classically trained chef with years of experience working at some of the best new American kitchens in New York City, including my own twelve-year-old Brooklyn restaurant called the Good Fork. But those flavors of home—piled up on that black lacquered table so long ago—are all I want to eat.

My mother (center) with friends at the party, enjoying the fruits of her labor

And so I opened my second restaurant, Insa, in 2015. It is 100 percent Korean—dedicated to traditional flavors, recreated and reinvented in small, subtle ways from what I have learned working as a professional chef. There's the traditional K-BBQ of sliced pork belly and *kalbi*, or marinated short ribs, to grill right at the tables. There's an array of Korean favorites like *soondae*, or blood sausage, plus crisp pan-fried pancakes with shrimp and squid, and the steamed pork belly called *bossam*. There is, of course, the ever-popular Korean fried chicken, aka KFC, and pan-fried *mandu*, or dumplings. There's also karaoke: It is meant to be a celebratory place, big and fun and boisterous.

But there is also joy in the more simplified way my family ate at home. When I was growing up, dinner was more often than not steamed mixed rice and grains, a simple bowl of kimchi stew or soup brought still bubbling to the table, plus banchan and maybe seasonal fruit to finish the meal. Everyone got a bowl of rice, a bowl of soup, and then the banchan was where the sharing happened. More special occasions meant *dwegi bulgogi* on the table, or a broiled beltfish, or a soup like *kalbi tang*, made with succulent braised short ribs. Occasionally my mother would make wonderfully rich Chinese-Korean dishes, like *jjajang myeon* or black bean noodles, or *kkanpoong saewoo*, our version of sweet-and-sour crispy fried shrimp.

For breakfast, we had leftover banchan over rice with gochujang sauce in *bibimbop*, or simply fried rice tossed with whatever was left over. Leftovers were also packed into our lunch boxes, with a little rice and banchan, plus the plain rolled omelet called *gyeran mari*, or the roasted seaweed and rice rolls called *kimbop*.

My father brought out all the furniture to the front yard, so we could sit together on this very special day.

Me, age 3, severely
squinting at the sun,
with my sisters, Jean
and Sue

I like to say Korean food is similar to southern Italian peasant food, as in we're working with just a few humble ingredients—in our case chile paste, soybean paste, soy sauce, rice wine vinegar, sesame oil, and seasonal vegetables, to name but a few—just combined in slightly different ways and with a knowing hand to make them different, and delicious.

In truth the greatest compliment I have received about my cooking was from my mom and aunt, who told me right before I opened the restaurant that I have good *sohn mat*. A Korean cook's talent is measured in her sohn mat: The literal translation is "taste of the hand." Someone who has good sohn mat has a deft hand with seasonings, yes, but is also someone who was born with a passion for food, who possesses the instinctive know-how to work with each ingredient on its own terms, and who can take a traditional recipe and make it their own.

That was really what was at the top of my mind when I opened Insa, and when I was working on this book. It was never my intention to impress diners or readers with that now-famous K-BBQ or KFC—though we sell a lot of them, and you'll find both recipes in this cookbook. Instead I want to introduce you to the seasonal, the homemade, the stewed and the pickled, the real Korean way of cooking, all made with as much sohn mat as I can muster.

Sohui Kim, 2018

THE KOREAN KITCHEN

My kitchen is always stocked with a handful of Korean ingredients and other tools that I rely on. These are the ones that you'll come across most often in this book. They are sold at any Korean market or grocery store, are widely available at most other Asian markets, and can be ordered online from HMart.com and of course Amazon, which makes the most hard-to-find ingredient available to almost anyone anywhere. Plus, these days, many Korean ingredients are found at large supermarkets or specialty food shops.

ASIAN PEAR
This should be called the Korean pear or *bae*, as it is originally from Korea. It's used in many marinades and sauces.

BAECHU (NAPA CABBAGE)
Look for tight, heavy heads without bruised leaves.

BUTCHU (GARLIC CHIVES)

MOO RADISH
Crisp, mild, firm, and sweet Korean radish. Daikon is a reasonable substitute if you can't find it.

RICE CAKES

KKETNIP
Also known as perilla or sesame leaves.

KOREAN GREEN CHILE
Fresh green Korean chiles, also called "long hots" or "long greens." They have mild to medium heat; if you can't find them, use jalapeño for pickled things, serranos for cooked dishes, and shishito peppers for braising and stewing.

SHISHITO PEPPERS

GOCHUGARU
Korean dried red pepper flakes made from the red, ripened form of Korean chile peppers. They are fully ripened on the plant, sun-dried and seeded, then ground into coarse or fine pepper. (*Gochu* means "chile pepper," and *garu* means "powder.") I use coarse flakes for kimchi and finer for things like banchan. It comes in many different levels of heat; check the intensity of yours before you use it. Store this long-term in the freezer, and use it within a year.

SHILGOCHU
Korean chile threads, sometimes labeled "red pepper sliced," store this in the freezer.

HOLLAND CHILE
Used primarily for their color, these are slightly sweeter than ripe, red versions of Korean green chiles, which are hard to find outside of Korea.

MYEON (NOODLES)

Memil Myeon (Buckwheat Noodles)

Naeng Myeon (Thin Mixed-Starch Chewy Noodles)

Dang Myeon (Sweet Potato Starch, aka Korean Vermicelli Noodles)

So Myeon (Dried Wheat Noodles)

Udon (Fresh Korean Noodles)

Jjeol Myeon (Thick Mixed-Starch Chewy Noodles)

DOENJANG

A salty, nutty, umami-packed Korean fermented soybean paste made by slowly simmering dried soybeans that are mashed into a paste and formed into bricks called *meju*, which are hung up to dry and ferment. The dried blocks are soaked in salt water in a stone crock to break down even further for months on end. You end up with both doenjang and *ganjang*, or Korean soy sauce. Darker, aged versions of doenjang are good for soup, while fresher lighter versions are better for the *ssam jang* on page 157. If you can't find doenjang, use a chunky dark miso paste.

GOCHUJANG

Korean red chile paste made of *gochugaru* (red chile flakes), sugar, glutinous rice, fermented soybeans, and salt, traditionally fermented together in earthenware pots for years. Order this online if you can't find it locally: There's really nothing you can use as a substitute. Store this and the doenjang in the refrigerator, and use them both within a year.

GLUTINOUS
(SWEET)
RICE FLOUR

ROASTED
SOYBEAN
POWDER

DRIED JUJUBES ("RED DATES")
Subtly sweet dried Eurasian berry that looks like a date

DRIED BRACKEN
(DRIED KOREAN FERN)

MOO MALLENG E
(DRIED MOO RADISH)

SHREDDED
DRIED SQUID/
CUTTLEFISH

LARGE DRIED
ANCHOVIES
For soup and stews

SMALL DRIED
ANCHOVIES
For stir-fries and banchan

DRIED
POLLACK
For soup

CURED
POLLACK
ROE

SALTED
SHRIMP

SILKEN
TOFU

FIRM
TOFU

MYEOK
For seaweed
soup and salad

ROASTED SALTED
SEAWEED
For snacking

NORI
(ROASTED SEAWEED)

BUGAK(CRISPY FRIED
SEAWEED CHIPS)
Dried and ready for
frying as per page 59

SHREDDED
ROASTED
SEAWEED
For garnishing

DASHIMA OR
KOMBU
(DRIED KELP)

SWEET GLUTINOUS RICE
Not to be confused
with Thai sticky rice,
though you could use it
in a pinch

MILLET

DRIED
SOY-
BEANS

BLACK
RICE

SHORT-GRAIN
WHITE RICE

MIXED DRY
BEANS
To soak
and cook
with rice

TOASTED
SESAME
SEEDS

ADZUKI BEANS

PEELED, SPLIT
MUNG BEANS

SHORT-GRAIN
BROWN RICE

SEORITAE
(BLACK
SOYBEANS)

TOASTED
BLACK
SESAME
SEEDS

WIRE MESH
INFUSERS
For spices
and aromatics
in broth

SPIDER
A wire-
mesh
strainer
for fried
things and
cooked
noodles

RICE
WINE
VINEGAR

BROWN
RICE
SYRUP

SOY
SAUCE

TOASTED
PERILLA
SEED

FISH
SAUCE

WHITE
SOY
SAUCE

SESAME
OIL

MINI
GRATER
For
ginger
and
garlic

POINTED
HOLE GRATER
For grating
Asian pear
and onion

HOW TO CUT A
VEGETABLE INTO JULIENNE

1.

Slice vegetable in half
lengthwise. Then cut it
into ⅛-inch (3 mm) half-
moon slices, making sure to
keep the sliced lined up.

2.

Fan out the slices across
your cutting board.

3.

Cut the fanned slices into
⅛-inch (3 mm) strips, working your way along the fan.

HOW TO CUT
SCALLIONS INTO STRIPS

1.

Trim off the root ends.

2.

Halve the whites length-
wise. If the scallions are
very large, quarter them.

3.

Cut the scallions into
2-inch (5 cm) strips.

HOW TO
COOK RICE

HOW TO
SOAK SEAWEED

1. There are many ways to make rice, and this is how I do it—it works with any kind of rice. You want to end up with about 1 cup (184 g) rice per person, so start with ½ cup (100 g) uncooked rice per person

Cut the seaweed into small pieces and soak it in warm water for 20 minutes, then drain and use in soups and salads.

2. Rinse and clean the rice in cold water at least three times, or until the water runs clear. Put the rice in the pot you are going to cook it in, and then cover the rice with cold water. Place your clean hand in the pot and lay it flat on top of the rice with your fingers spread out as shown. The water should just cover your knuckles. If it doesn't, add a little more; if it's too much, pour a little out. (This I call my grandma trick, because it's how my grandmother taught me.)

HOW TO CUT
EGG RIBBONS

3. Cover the pot tightly and bring the water to a boil. Reduce the heat to as low as you can go without it being off, and cook for 18 minutes without lifting the lid. After 18 minutes, increase the heat to high for 1 minute without lifting the lid, then turn off the heat and let the pot sit covered for 15 minutes more. Remove the lid, fluff the rice, and keep it covered and warm until time to serve.

Make a thin flat omelet; then move it to a cutting board and use a sharp knife to cut it into thick or thin slices.

Every Korean meal begins with *banchan*! The word means "small dishes," but banchan is so much more than shared sides: It is the heart of Korean cooking. They are a requirement at every meal, even a bowl of noodles—in many cases banchan *is* the meal: You pick up a little banchan with your chopsticks, put it on your bowl of rice for flavor and texture, and that's dinner. On normal nights, most people have at least two or three banchan; for more formal dinners, the table could have a dozen or more. Banchan is about sharing, and even love: Some people say they know which child is the mother's favorite by how many banchan they put on their rice when they were too young to do it themselves.

You should approach banchan the same way you'd think about composing the menu for a dinner party—in other words, you want variation. In a perfect world, you'd have an array of things that might be pickled, braised, cooked, fresh, fried, light, heavy, spicy, refreshing, seasonal, cold, hot, or room temperature, not to mention a rainbow of colors.

That's why it's handy to remember that banchan doesn't always have to be a platter stuffed with pan-fried vegetable patties or a bowl of time-intensive kimchi (the latter counts as both banchan and all-purpose condiment). You could serve a lot of one bright fresh salad, but one bite per person of something decadent. Banchan can also be less complicated than the recipes here: They could be leftover sautéed vegetables, sliced fresh chiles, or whatever you like: leftovers from soup or stew or fried chicken or broiled fish, sliced and served for the table. You can really turn almost anything in this book into banchan—just cut it up, season it a bit, then add it to the table.

BANCHAN
VEGETABLES & SIDES

BANCHAN 101

I grouped this chapter into seven major types of banchan: *jorim*, *jeon*, *twigim*, *bokkeum*, *namul*, *muchim*, and *kimchi*. If you're planning a meal, be sure to serve at least a few different styles. A note on serving banchan: Traditionally it is served as just a few bites in small bowls that can be easily passed around the table, then refilled as needed. You can serve it in one big platter or bowl, if you like; just make sure it is wide and flat, so you can reach across the table and grab the contents with your chopsticks. For the same reason, all banchan are cut into pieces you can easily maneuver with your chopsticks.

JORIM

Jorim means "stewed" or "braised," as in slow-cooking meats or vegetables in a reduced sauce as a way to preserve them and add flavor. The most common form is soy-braised, because soy sauce is salty, helping to further preserve whatever you jorim.

JEON

Jeon means something like "patty"—these are soft, pan-fried things like savory pancakes and omelets.

TWIGIM

Deep-fried and crunchy.

BOKKEUM

Stir-fried.

NAMUL

This is light vegetable banchan—*namul* basically means "seasoned greens." These are also often best mixed by hand.

MUCHIM

Muchim is both banchan and a technique. The word roughly means "to toss things with your hands," and it's a key component of *sohn mat*, or "taste of the hand," because you can feel when things are seasoned to your liking.

KIMCHI

Kimchi—basically salted and fermented vegetables—is the national dish of Korea, the thing everyone knows about the country, and it really takes center stage in our cuisine.

Kimchi is the king of banchan, an all-purpose condiment, a seasoning, a side, a topping, and a way to preserve foods and make them even healthier thanks to real-deal lacto-fermentation.

UNESCO has even declared *kimjang*—the communal act of making kimchi with your village and family in the fall so that everyone has enough through winter—an "intangible cultural property." My father used to say kimchi ran in his veins, and I agree: If I don't have kimchi for a while, I feel unwell. He also used to say, "If you don't have kimchi on the table, you're not eating well."

Jorim

(Braised)

YUN-GEUN JORIM

GLAZED LOTUS ROOT

Though we call this vegetable lotus root, technically what we're eating is the lotus rhizome, or the semi-hollow, crunchy stems of the lotus flower. (You've seen their beautiful pink-white blooms among the lily pads in tropical ponds.) The stems, which are similar in feel to water chestnuts, grow underwater in connected series of orange-pink pods. You peel the skin and slice the off-white flesh into lacy coins with a distinctive hole-y appearance. Here they are braised until tender, but still crunchy, and coated with a wonderful sticky, salty, sweet glaze.

NOTE: You should be able to find lotus "root" pods at almost any Asian grocery with a produce section. If you can't find them, good substitutes are burdock root or parsnips.

Serves 4

1 pound (455 g)
  lotus root
  (see Note)

2 teaspoons rice
  wine vinegar

1 tablespoon
  olive oil

⅓ cup (75 ml)
  soy sauce

3 tablespoons
  packed brown
  sugar

⅓ cup (75 ml)
  brown rice syrup

1 tablespoon
  toasted sesame
  seeds

1 Peel the lotus root and slice it into ¼-inch (6 mm) rounds.

2 Put the lotus root slices in a medium saucepan with 4 cups (960 ml) water (add more if necessary to cover) and add the vinegar. Bring the liquid to a boil and let the lotus root simmer for 10 minutes.

3 Drain the lotus root and rinse it well in cold water until the slices feel cool to the touch. Shake off any excess water and let the slices drain in a colander over the sink or a bowl.

4 Clean and dry your saucepan and heat the oil over medium heat. Add the soy sauce, sugar, and 1½ cups (360 ml) water and let it come to a low boil, increasing the heat if necessary.

5 Add the cooked lotus root and cook them in the sugar-soy mixture, stirring occasionally, until the sauce has reduced by a little more than half, about 12 to 15 minutes.

6 Stir in the rice syrup and keep moving the lotus root slices in the pan so that every piece is glazed with the sauce. Let the lotus root cook until it is tender, about 20 minutes more. If the pot gets dry, add 1 or 2 tablespoons water.

7 Stir in the sesame seeds and serve hot, at room temperature, or chilled. This will keep in the refrigerator for about 1 week.

JANG JORIM

SOY-BRAISED BEEF

Think of this beef *banchan*—which is almost always eaten cold or at room temperature—as less like a traditional beef stew and more like a preserve or a pickle. This was traditionally a way to use up scraps of meat, cooking them down in a wonderful sauce both to make them more flavorful and to preserve them. You really want the liquid to reduce and become infused with the flavor of the meat and aromatics. While you could remove the seeds from all those chiles for less heat, I don't: They give the sauce a nice kick that really makes this dish. Korean green chiles are traditional, but I often use shishito peppers because I like the sweet, floral, slightly spicy notes, and they taste good stewed. You could eat this hot right after you make it as a meal, if you like, but traditionally this is served cold after an overnight rest to let the flavors develop.

NOTE: You don't need to remove all the fat from the beef, but if it's very thick in spots, trim it slightly.

Strain the meat and aromatics from the stock after the beef is done, and presto! You have concentrated Korean beef stock.

Serves 4 to 6

FOR THE BEEF AND STOCK

- 2 pounds (910 g) beef brisket or chuck, cut into 2-inch (5 cm) chunks (see Note)
- ½ medium yellow onion, quartered
- 2 scallions, cut into thirds
- 8 cloves garlic, halved
- 2-inch (5 cm/25 g) piece peeled fresh ginger, halved

FOR THE SEASONING

- ⅓ cup (75 ml) soy sauce
- 2 tablespoons granulated sugar
- 2 tablespoons rice wine vinegar
- 1 (4 inch/10 cm) square piece kombu seaweed
- 5 Korean green chiles or shishito peppers, sliced 1 inch (2.5 cm) thick

1   In a medium saucepan, cover the beef, onion, scallions, garlic, and ginger with 4 cups (960 ml) water and bring to a simmer. Partially cover the pot and let it cook for 1½ hours.

2   Add the soy sauce, sugar, rice wine vinegar, kombu, and chiles to the saucepan. Let everything simmer, uncovered, for 20 minutes.

3   Let the pot cool, then cover and refrigerate overnight.

4   The next day, skim off the fat that has risen to the top and discard it. Then use your clean hands to shred the beef.

5   Serve cold or at room temperature by placing some of the shredded beef in a bowl with a little of the sauce, along with some of the chiles, onions, ginger, and scallions, if you like. It will last in the fridge for up to a week.

GAMJA JORIM

POTATO STEWED IN SOY SAUCE

There are as many ways to make this as there are Korean cooks—everyone tinkers with the ratio of soy sauce, water, and sweetness. This is my approach: neither too sweet nor too salty. I prefer to use Yukon gold potatoes because I love their buttery, creamy flavor and they hold their texture better than starchier russets, which are the traditional choice. You can really use any type of potato you have—the trick is just to soak and rinse them multiple times to get rid of excess starch. Though this will last for a day or two, it tastes best the day it is made, before refrigeration.

Serves 6 to 8

- 2 pounds (910 g) potatoes, cut into 1-inch (2.5 cm) chunks
- 3 tablespoons olive oil
- ½ large white onion, cut into 1-inch (2.5 cm) pieces
- 2 tablespoons soy sauce
- 2 tablespoons graulated sugar
- 1 tablespoon honey
- 1 teaspoon sesame oil
- 1 teaspoon toasted sesame seeds

1 In a mixing bowl, cover the potatoes with cold water and let them soak for 30 minutes. Then rinse them three times in clean water and drain.

2 In a large skillet, heat the olive oil over medium-high heat, then add the onions and potatoes. Let them cook, stirring often, for about 1 minute, making sure the onions don't brown. Then stir in 1 cup (240 ml) water, the soy sauce, and the sugar.

3 Reduce the heat to medium and let everything simmer, stirring occasionally, until the water evaporates into a syrupy consistency.

4 After 10 minutes, add the honey and check the texture of the potatoes. If the water has evaporated but the potatoes are not cooked through, add ¼ cup (60 ml) water and let it come to a simmer, then turn off the heat. Taste for seasoning and add more soy sauce as needed.

5 Stir in the sesame oil and sesame seeds and let cool. Serve cold or at room temperature. This will last in the refrigerator for 1 to 2 days.

DAE-PA JORIM

CHARRED BRAISED LEEKS

This is not a traditional Korean *banchan*, but I just knew it would taste good. And how could it not, with charred sweet leeks slow-cooked in anchovy stock and umami-rich *doenjang*? If you have a bunch of leeks on hand, this is *the* recipe for them.

These braised beauties are also perfect as a side dish to steak and mashed potatoes. After the leeks are cooked, reduce the braising liquid a little in the pan and swirl in some butter till it melts to make the most delicious steak sauce.

Serves 4

1 pound (455 g/about 2 large) leeks

1 tablespoon canola oil

Kosher salt

2 cups (480 ml) Master Anchovy Stock (page 228)

2 teaspoons soy sauce

1 tablespoon doenjang

1   Split the leeks lengthwise, trimming the root but leaving enough stem intact that the leeks still hold together. Immerse the leeks in cold running water and make sure they are clean of any grit or dirt between the leaves.

2   Pat the leeks very dry, discard the dark green tops, and cut the white and light green parts into 2 to 3 pieces.

3   In a skillet, heat the oil over high heat. When it begins to smoke, place the leeks in the pan cut side down and let them char and caramelize, turning so both sides are browned, about a minute and a half to 2 minutes per side. You may need to do this in batches. (You just want color here—no need to fully cook them.)

4   In a medium saucepan, bring the anchovy stock, soy sauce, and doenjang to a boil. Add the charred leeks, lower the heat, and let them cook for 8 minutes at a low simmer.

5   Serve the leeks hot, at room temperature, or even chilled with a little of the braising liquid. They will last in the refrigerator for 2 to 3 days.

DUBU JORIM

SOY-BRAISED TOFU

Banchan favorite among Koreans. You can boost the spiciness with even more *gochugaru*, or red chile flakes, if you are so inclined. The sweet spot for this dish is the day after you make it: It is even better after the tofu absorbs the sauce. The trick is not to make the dish too salty, because you're reducing the soy sauce: Don't add any more salt or soy sauce to taste until the sauce has finished cooking.

Serves 4

2 tablespoons
  soy sauce

½ teaspoon
  granulated sugar

½ teaspoon
  gochugaru (or
  more, if desired)

2 tablespoons
  thinly sliced
  scallions

1 teaspoon
  minced garlic

3 tablespoons
  grapeseed or
  olive oil

1 pound (455 g) firm
  tofu,
  patted dry and
  sliced ½ inch
  (12 mm) thick

2 teaspoons
  sesame oil

Pinch shilgochu
  (Korean chile
  threads)

1 teaspoon toasted
  sesame seeds,
  for garnish

1   In a small mixing bowl, combine the soy sauce, sugar, gochugaru, scallions, and garlic with ½ cup (120 ml) water. Set this aside while you brown the tofu.

2   In your largest skillet, heat half of the oil over medium heat. Cook the tofu slices flat in the pan, leaving a little bit of space in between, until both sides are lightly browned, about 3 minutes per side. Add the remaining oil when you flip the slices over.

3   Add the soy sauce mixture to the pan. Let it simmer over medium to medium-high heat, basting the tofu often with the liquid, until it reduces slightly, about 2 to 3 minutes.

4   Turn off the heat and stir in the sesame oil and the chile threads, and garnish with the sesame seeds. Serve hot, at room temperature, or chilled. This can be stored in the refrigerator for 2 to 3 days.

GYERAN JORIM

SOY-MARINATED SEVEN-MINUTE EGGS

These seven-minute eggs are beautiful—and yummy—on their own as *banchan*, or even a snack, sliced open to reveal the layers of color from their spicy-sweet soy marinade. They can also be added to Jang Jorim (page 22), Bibimbop (page 246), or any of the noodle dishes in this book. You want the chiles you use to be just a little hot, like Mexican chiles de árbol. You can make this with just soy sauce and water, which is traditional, but the brine here has more flavor and much less salt: I wanted to be able to eat the brine on rice or to braise vegetables or meats or tofu for another *jorim*. (A soy-only brine, by the way, will color the eggs in just 10 minutes.)

```
You don't have to
use Korean soy sauce
(ganjang) for the
recipes in this
book, but be sure
to buy one that is
"naturally brewed"
rather than created
in a lab and filled
with caramel coloring
or preservatives.
With real brewed soy
sauce, you taste the
complexity of the soy,
not just salt.
```

Makes 6 eggs

```
6 large eggs
¾ cup (180 ml)
  soy sauce
3 tablespoons mirin
2 tablespoons rice
  wine vinegar
3 dried chile
  peppers, such as
  chiles de árbol
5 cloves garlic,
  peeled
Toasted sesame
  seeds, for garnish
  (optional)
```

1   Bring a large saucepan of water to a boil and prepare a large mixing bowl full of ice water.

2   Gently lower the eggs into the pot of boiling water and let them cook for 7 minutes. Remove them from the pot immediately to the bowl of ice water. Use your hand to gently crack each egg slightly against the side of the bowl as you add them.

3   When the eggs are cool enough to handle, peel them and set them aside in a clean bowl of cold water.

4   In a large saucepan, bring the soy sauce, mirin, rice wine vinegar, chile peppers, and garlic to a boil with 2 cups (480 ml) water. Lower the heat and let the liquid cook at a simmer for 5 minutes.

5   Turn off the heat and add the eggs to the pot. Remove them when the whites of the eggs have taken on color, about 1 hour, reserving the brine for another use, if desired. Alternatively, you can simply store them in the brine in the refrigerator overnight and then drain off the liquid the next day.

6   Serve the eggs chilled or at room temperature. Slice them into quarters or halves and dust their tops with the sesame seeds, if desired. They can be stored in the refrigerator for 3 to 4 days.

GOGUMA JORIM

ROASTED SWEET POTATOES

Like braised leeks (see page 26), these are not a traditional Korean *banchan*—for starters there is very little roasting in our cooking, because historically we didn't have ovens, and the pickled jalapeños are obviously borrowed from Mexico. I also use the orange American-style sweet potatoes here, rather than traditional white ones like those found in Korea, as I think their sweetness just goes so well with kimchi. In truth, this banchan is a cross between a *jorim*, or braise, and a *muchim*, or tossed salad. Though this will last for a day or two, it tastes best at room temperature the day it is made, before refrigeration.

Serves 6 to 8

2 pounds (910 g)
  sweet potatoes

2 tablespoons
  olive oil

Kosher salt

¼ cup (60 ml) rice
  wine vinegar

2 teaspoons
  sesame oil

2 teaspoons
  gochugaru

2 teaspoons
  soy sauce

1 teaspoon
  minced garlic

¾ cup (45 g) thinly
  sliced scallions

¼ cup (40 g)
  thinly sliced
  pickled jalapeños
  (optional)

1   Preheat the oven to 425°F (220°C).

2   Scrub the sweet potatoes clean and cut them into 1-inch (2.5 cm) cubes.

3   In a mixing bowl, toss the sweet potato cubes with the olive oil and a pinch of salt, then lay them out on a baking sheet.

4   Roast the sweet potatoes for about 20 minutes, or until cooked through and crispy on the outside. Let cool.

5   In a mixing bowl, toss the cooled sweet potatoes with the vinegar, sesame oil, gochugaru, soy sauce, garlic, scallions, and pickled peppers, if using. Serve at room temperature or cold. It will last in the refrigerator for 1 to 2 days.

DAN HOBAK JORIM

SWEET SOY-GLAZED KABOCHA

Traditionally you would just cook the squash in a pot with the seasonings to make this dish, but you coax a lot more sweetness out of the squash when you roast it just until tender first—*dan hobak* means "sweet squash," after all. Though you can peel the squash with a vegetable peeler, I leave the skin on, as it is full of nutrients and good nutty flavor. Just scrub it well and remove any warts and such. If you can't find kabocha, you could use butternut, but be careful when you roast it—butternut squash has a higher water content and can turn to mush more quickly.

Serves 4 to 6

1 kabocha squash (about 2 pounds/ 910 g), well scrubbed

Olive oil, for greasing

½ cup (110 g) packed brown sugar

⅓ cup (75 ml) soy sauce

¼ cup (60 ml) mirin

3 tablespoons rice wine vinegar

2 tablespoons sesame oil

Toasted salted pumpkin seeds, for garnish

1 Preheat the oven to 425°F (220°C).

2 Cut the squash in half and remove the seeds. Lightly coat the squash halves inside and out with olive oil and roast cut side up on a baking sheet for about 35 minutes, or just until the squash is easily pierced with the tip of a knife. (If you overcook it, the squash gets mushy; you can still eat it, but it's nicer when it's a bit firm.) Remove from the oven.

3 When the squash is cool enough to handle, cut it into 2-inch (5 cm) chunks.

4 In a large skillet or medium saucepan, heat the brown sugar with ¼ cup (60 ml) water and the soy sauce, mirin, and vinegar over medium heat, stirring until the sugar dissolves. Let it simmer for about 2 to 3 minutes, then stir in the kabocha pieces, tossing them in the mixture until they are well coated.

5 To serve right away or within a few hours at room temperature, put the squash in a serving dish, then drizzle with the sesame oil and sprinkle with toasted pumpkin seeds. It can also be stored in the refrigerator for 3 to 4 days and eaten chilled, but don't add the sesame oil or pumpkin seeds until you're ready to serve it.

KONGJANG

SOY-BRAISED BLACK SOYBEANS

This dish, also called *kongjaban*, is a real crowd-pleaser, though non-Koreans do have to get used to the fact that these pitch-black soybeans retain their texture so that they are almost al dente: They should have a real bite. It can be surprising to those expecting traditional beans, normally cooked until soft. You will need to find *seoritae*, or dried black soybeans, which are available at Korean markets, some natural food stores, and online. Just don't try to use regular dried black beans, which will get mushy.

Serves 6 to 8

2 cups (340 g)
    seoritae (dried
    black soybeans)

½ cup (120 ml)
    soy sauce

¼ cup (50 g)
    granulated sugar

1 to 2 tablespoons
    brown rice syrup

1 teaspoon toasted
    sesame seeds,
    for garnish

1   Rinse the dried beans several times in cold running water, picking through them to discard any stones or broken beans. Put the beans in a medium saucepan and pour in 2 cups (480 ml) water, or enough to cover the beans by about an inch (2.5 cm). Let them soak for about 30 minutes.

2   Drain the beans and rinse them once or twice in cold water. Then pour in another 2 cups (480 ml) water, or enough to cover the beans by about an inch (2.5 cm).

3   Bring the beans to a boil over high heat, then reduce the heat to medium and let them simmer for 12 minutes.

4   Add the soy sauce and sugar and let everything simmer for 30 minutes more, or until the liquid has reduced by half. Check the beans to see if they are done: They should be soft, but with a little bit of bite to them. If they're not done, let them cook for a few minutes more.

5   When the beans are ready, stir in the rice syrup and adjust the soy sauce or syrup to taste. Let the beans cool in the pot, then garnish with the sesame seeds and serve at room temperature or cold. They will keep in the refrigerator for 2 to 3 weeks.

HOBAK JEON

GREEN SQUASH FRITTERS

Jeon

(Pan-Fried)

A classic, go-to *jeon* for *banchan*. In fact, think of this recipe as a technique, not a dish: You can substitute almost anything you can easily pan-fry—beef, seafood, tofu pieces, sweet potatoes—all thinly sliced so you fry them consistently, and all served with a dipping sauce. Every jeon needs a good dipping sauce, even if it's just a little soy sauce sweetened with rice wine vinegar.

NOTE: You can usually find Korean green squash in the produce department of Korean grocery stores. They look like pale green versions of zucchini, but they are sturdier and firmer. If you don't have access to them, regular yellow crookneck squash or Mexican squash (sometimes called avocado squash) are good substitutes. Zucchini can work if you can't find either.

Serves 4

FOR THE JEON
DIPPING SAUCE

3 tablespoons
   soy sauce

2 tablespoons rice
   wine vinegar

1 teaspoon
   gochugaru

½ teaspoon toasted
   sesame seeds

FOR THE FRITTERS

1 pound (455 g)
   Korean green or
   crookneck squash
   (see Note)

⅓ cup (40 g)
   all-purpose flour

Kosher salt

2 large eggs

¼ cup (60 ml)
   canola oil

1 Make the dipping sauce: In a small mixing bowl, whisk together the soy sauce, vinegar, gochugaru, and sesame seeds. Set this aside while you make the squash.

2 Make the fritters: Slice the squash into ½-inch (12 mm) slices.

3 Mix the flour with ¼ teaspoon salt in a small mixing bowl. In a large mixing bowl, beat the eggs with 1 teaspoon salt.

4 In a large skillet or frying pan, heat the oil over medium-low heat until it begins to shimmer.

5 While the oil heats, dredge the squash slices in the flour, tapping them on the side of the bowl to remove excess flour, and set them on a plate or baking sheet.

6 When the oil is hot, work quickly to dip the squash slices in the egg so that they are completely covered on all sides, and then add them to the frying pan in a single layer.

7 Fry the slices until they are golden brown on the bottom, about 2 minutes. Be sure to watch the heat carefully as you fry: You want it to be hot enough so that there are bubbles around the edges of the squash, but you don't want the egg to get too brown or it will taste bitter. Flip the squash and cook for another 2 minutes, or until the other side is golden brown and the squash is cooked through and tender. (They'll be slightly soft when you press down with your finger or a pair of tongs.)

8 Remove the squash to a plate with a pair of tongs and serve hot or at room temperature with small bowls of jeon dipping sauce.

KKETNIP JEON

STUFFED PERILLA LEAVES

I love this kind of *jeon*, or stuffed finger food–type things—they are my favorite *banchan* type. These stuffed perilla leaves use a sausage filling, but you could do this with tuna, beef, or pork. You could also stuff seeded Korean green peppers with this mix, or even make little meatballs. If you can't find perilla leaves, you can substitute Japanese shiso, though they tend to be smaller and are more delicate—for this dish it's worth seeking out the real thing. For the sausages, any already seasoned pork sausage that isn't strongly flavored, like mild Italian, is fine.

Serves 4 to 6

FOR THE FILLING

½ cup (55 g) minced white onion

12 ounces (340 g) pork sausage, casings removed

2 teaspoons minced garlic

1 large egg, beaten

¼ teaspoon freshly ground black pepper

¼ cup (20 g) panko breadcrumbs

Kosher salt

FOR STUFFING AND FRYING THE LEAVES

½ cup (65 g) all-purpose flour

3 large eggs, beaten

12 to 16 large perilla or shiso leaves (about 1 ounce/28 g), washed and dried

¼ cup (60 ml) olive or canola oil

Haemul Pajeon Dipping Sauce (page 44)

1   Make the filling: In a small mixing bowl, combine the onion, sausage, garlic, egg, black pepper, panko, and a tiny pinch of salt. (You shouldn't need much, as the sausage is already seasoned.) Mix everything well with your hands. Set aside.

2   Stuff and fry the leaves: Place the flour in one small mixing bowl and the eggs in another. Take a leaf, and if it is large, remove the stem because it is tough. Dredge the leaf in the flour.

3   Take 2 tablespoons of meat mixture and use a spoon to roughly spread it on one side of the leaf, then fold the leaf in half around the filling so the two edges are pressed together into a half-moon shape. Be sure to flatten the mixture inside by pressing down to about ¼ inch (6 mm). (If you have a small leaf, use less filling.) Set the leaf aside on a cutting board and repeat until all are filled.

4   Dip each stuffed leaf into the beaten egg so that all sides are covered, and set it aside on a baking sheet.

5   In large nonstick skillet or cast-iron frying pan, heat the oil over medium-low heat.

6   Lay the leaves down flat in the pan, making sure they don't touch. (You can fry these in batches, if need be.)

7   Flip them when the bottoms are brown, after about a minute. After the other side has browned, keep flipping from time to time so the filling cooks through and the leaves and egg batter don't burn, lowering your heat if necessary, another 3 or 4 minutes. The leaves should feel firm when the pork is done. The important thing here is not color but to make sure the meat is cooked through.

8   When the stuffed leaves are done, remove them to paper towels and serve hot or at room temperature with the dipping sauce on the side.

DWEJIGOGI JEON

PORK PATTIES

This is a hearty *jeon* that is
perfectly balanced and seasoned
on its own, but it is even better
dipped in a simple soy vinaigrette.
You can also make these patties
with ground beef.

Makes 16 (2-inch/5 cm) round patties

1 pound (455 g)
  ground pork

6 ounces (170 g)
  soft tofu

3 large eggs

1 teaspoon minced
  garlic

1 teaspoon minced
  peeled fresh
  ginger

1 tablespoon soy
  sauce, plus more
  for dipping

⅓ cup (20 g) thinly
  sliced scallions

⅓ cup (25 g) panko
  breadcrumbs

1 teaspoon
  kosher salt

1 teaspoon
  freshly ground
  black pepper

2 tablespoons
  grapeseed or
  olive oil

  Hobak Jeon
  Dipping Sauce
  (Page 39)

1   In a large mixing bowl, combine the pork,
    tofu, one of the eggs, garlic, ginger, soy
    sauce, scallions, panko, salt, and pepper.
    Mix well and set aside.

2   In a smaller bowl, beat together the
    remaining 2 eggs.

3   Form about 3 tablespoons of the meat
    mixture into a patty about 2 inches
    (5 cm) in diameter and ½ inch (12 mm)
    thick, placing it on a plate or baking
    sheet. Repeat until all the meat mixture
    has been formed into patties.

4   Dip each patty into the beaten egg,
    turning it so it is covered on both sides,
    then place it back on the plate or baking
    sheet.

5   In a skillet, heat the oil over medium heat.
    Add the patties a few at a time, making
    sure there is space in between them.
    (You will need to cook them in batches.)
    Cook the patties for 2 to 3 minutes on one
    side, or until they are golden brown, then
    flip them over and let them cook about 2
    minutes more, or until the other side is
    golden brown.

6   Transfer the patties to paper towels until
    all are done, then serve immediately with
    dipping sauce.

HAEMUL PAJEON

SEAFOOD PANCAKES WITH SCALLIONS AND CHILES

Koreans make savory pancakes, or *jeon*, with all kinds of ingredients, and my favorite are those filled with chopped shrimp, sliced squid, chiles, and lots and lots of scallions. (*Pa* means "scallions," so *pajeon* is "scallion pancakes.") For any jeon, a nicely balanced dipping sauce is key. Eat these as soon as you make them, while fresh, hot, and still crisp around the edges.

```
Koreans like to eat
pajeon on rainy days
with makgeolli, or
unfiltered fermented
rice drink. I agree
that makgeolli is a
great pairing, but you
don't need to wait for
bad weather to enjoy it!
```

Makes 2 (8-inch/20 cm) pancakes

FOR THE DIPPING SAUCE

- 2 tablespoons soy sauce
- 1 tablespoon rice wine vinegar
- ½ teaspoon gochugaru
- 1 teaspoon sesame oil
- 1 teaspoon toasted sesame seeds
- 1 scallion, thinly sliced

FOR THE PANCAKES

- ½ cup (75 g) potato starch
- ½ cup (75 g) all-purpose flour
- 1 teaspoon kosher salt
- ½ teaspoon baking powder
- 1 cup (240 ml) ice-cold water or seltzer
- 1 cup (6 ounces/ 150 g) shrimp, about 8 large
- 1 cup (7 ounces/ 200 g) thinly sliced squid, tentacles separated and quartered
- 2 scallions, thinly sliced
- 1 Korean green chile, seeded and sliced
- ¼ cup (60 ml) grapeseed or olive oil

1 Make the dipping sauce: In a small mixing bowl, whisk together the soy sauce, vinegar, gochugaru, sesame oil, toasted sesame seeds, and scallion. Set aside.

2 Make the pancakes: In a mixing bowl, combine the potato starch, flour, salt, baking powder, and cold water until well incorporated.

3 Fold in the shrimp, squid, scallions, and chile. Let this sit while you heat the oil.

4 In a skillet, heat 2 tablespoons of the oil over medium-high heat. When the pan is hot, add half of the batter to the pan and, working quickly, use the back of a spoon to spread the batter out on the bottom of the pan. Let the pancake cook for about 5 minutes on each side, or until slightly browned and crisp around the edges.

5 Cut the pancake into 8 pieces and serve immediately with the dipping sauce on the side.

6 Repeat steps 4 and 5 with the remaining oil and batter.

KIMCHI JEON

KIMCHI PANCAKES

These pancakes are another way to use up funky kimchi—I love them because they're tart and so savory. The leaves melt into the batter, but then you get a little crunchy bite of cabbage, which is the best part. You just need to add a little sweetness to the dipping sauce, because the pancakes themselves are a little tart. These are really best served right after you cook them, so the edges are still crispy. Typically you add a little cooked pork to these, as it is a great complement to kimchi, but shrimp are also delicious.

Makes 2 (5-inch/12 cm) pancakes

FOR THE
DIPPING SAUCE

1 tablespoon
  soy sauce

2 teaspoons rice
  wine vinegar

1 teaspoon honey

1 teaspoon toasted
  sesame seeds

FOR THE
PANCAKES

¼ cup (40 g)
  potato starch

½ cup (65 g)
  all-purpose flour

¼ teaspoon
  kosher salt

1 cup (150 g) Baechu
  Kimchi (page
  102), chopped

3 tablespoons
  kimchi juice

1 scallion, halved
  lengthwise and
  cut into ½-inch
  (12 mm) pieces

½ cup (120 ml)
  ice-cold water

1 large egg

½ cup (2 ounces/
  70 g) cooked meat,
  such as pork,
  bacon, chicken,
  or shrimp
  (optional)

¼ cup (60 ml)
  grapeseed or
  olive oil

1   Make the dipping sauce: In a small mixing bowl, whisk together the soy sauce, rice wine vinegar, honey, and sesame seeds. Set this aside while you make the pancakes.

2   Make the pancakes: In a large mixing bowl, combine the potato starch, flour, and salt. Add the kimchi, kimchi juice, scallion, ice-cold water, egg, and meat, if using, and mix until well combined.

3   Heat 1 tablespoon of the oil in an 8-inch (20 cm) nonstick pan over medium heat. Pour in half of the batter and let it cook for 3 minutes, or until the edges are crispy. Flip it over, add another tablespoon of oil, and let cook for another 3 minutes. Add another tablespoon of oil if the pan becomes very dry.

4   Cut into wedges or small pieces and serve immediately with the dipping sauce on the side.

5   Repeat steps 3 and 4 with the remaining oil and batter. (Alternatively, you can wait and serve them both at the same time, but they will lose their crispiness.)

BINDAETTEOK

MUNG BEAN PANCAKES WITH KIMCHI AND SPROUTS

I have dream-like memories of eating these pancakes on hiking trips as a young kid in Korea. Just off the trails you have many entrepreneurs in makeshift stalls selling food. They usually add cooked bacon or pork, and if you have some—or any other cooked protein, vegetable, or fresh herb—on hand, by all means add it. The split mung beans for *bindaetteok* are yellow because the beans are hulled before they are split. In Korea, there is also a version of this pancake called *nokdujeon* made with unhulled mung beans, which are green.

NOTE: Before you cook with them, you should cover both the mung beans and the soybeans with 3 inches (8 cm) water and soak for at least 3 hours at room temperature or overnight in the refrigerator.

Makes about 20 small pancakes

¼ cup (50 g) glutinous (sweet) rice flour

3 cups mung bean or soybean sprouts

2 cups split yellow mung beans, soaked and drained (see Note)

½ cup soybeans, soaked and drained (See Note)

1 tablespoon minced garlic

1 tablespoon minced peeled fresh ginger

2 tablespoons minced Korean red chile

2 cups (300 g) chopped Baechu Kimchi (page 102) with juice

1 cup (55 g) diced scallions

1 tablespoon kosher salt

Grapeseed or olive oil, for pan-frying

Kimchi Jeon Dipping Sauce (page 47)

1   Soak the glutinous rice flour in 1 cup (240 ml) water while you prep everything else.

2   Bring a pot of lightly salted water to a boil and prepare a bowl of lightly salted ice water. Blanch the sprouts by dropping them into the boiling water, then immediately remove them to the bowl of ice water. Move them around with your clean hands until all the sprouts are cooled. Drain immediately and squeeze all the water out with your hands. Place them in a colander set over a bowl to continue to drain while you make the pancake batter.

3   Rinse the drained soaked mung beans and soybeans and place them in a food processor or blender along with the rice flour and its soaking water. Process until the beans are mostly smooth but still have a few chunks—you want the pancakes to have some texture.

4   Transfer the bean mixture to a large mixing bowl and add the garlic, ginger, chile, kimchi with juice, blanched mung bean sprouts, scallions, and 2 cups (480 ml) water. Add the salt and stir everything together until it is well mixed. The batter should look like loose porridge; if it looks dry, add up to ½ cup (120 ml) more water. Taste for salt.

5   In a skillet, heat 2 tablespoons oil over medium-high heat and pour in ¼ cup (60 ml) batter, flattening it slightly with the back of a spoon or spatula into a round pancake. (Cook as many pancakes as will fit in the pan at a time.) Fry the pancakes until they begin to brown and crisp around the edges. Flip them over and cook for another 3 to 4 minutes, or until the other side is browned and crisp, adding more oil if the pan looks dry.

6   Serve immediately with the dipping sauce on the side. Repeat steps 5 and 6 with the remaining batter.

GYERAN MARI

ROLLED OMELET WITH VEGETABLES

I always ask for refills of this *banchan* at Korean restaurants, and I usually get denied when I try for thirds. That's okay—it's very easy to make at home, and kids love it, too. You're basically making a multi-layered omelet: The sheets of roasted seaweed (see page 13) in between are optional, but they look so dramatic and add a little extra color and flavor. I usually make a few of these with seaweed and a few without. The recipe can be easily multiplied to make as many *gyeran* (egg) *mari* (roll) as you like.

NOTE: These are traditionally made in a special 7-inch (18 cm) rectangular nonstick pan with a flared lip so you can easily roll up the omelet. They're readily available online—just look for the words "rolled omelet pan." Do you have to use it? No. But if you're going to make a lot of these, it's worth the investment.

Makes 2 rolled omelets

5 large eggs

1 scallion,
   thinly sliced

2 tablespoons
   diced carrot

½ teaspoon
   kosher salt

Grapeseed or olive
   oil, for greasing

2 to 4 sheets of
   roasted seaweed,
   cut to fit the
   pan (optional)

1   In a mixing bowl, whisk the eggs until well beaten. Fold in the scallion, carrot, and salt.

2   Heat a small nonstick pan or square omelet pan (see Note) over low to medium-low heat. Add 1 teaspoon oil, blot the pan dry with paper towels, and carefully pour a very thin layer of egg batter (about ¼ cup/60 ml) into the pan.

3   If you are adding the seaweed, lay a sheet directly on top of the eggs when the eggs just begin to set around the edges.

4   After you add the seaweed, or once the eggs are just cooked through, use a flexible spatula to fold up the omelet until you get to one end and let it sit there. Add another thin layer of egg to the pan, and when it is almost set, lay down a second sheet of seaweed, if using.

5   Roll the second layer of omelet up around the first one, then set the omelet aside on a cutting board. Let it cool slightly before cutting it into ½-inch (12 mm) slices.

6   Repeat steps 2 to 5 to make the second omelet.

7   Serve the slices of omelet immediately, at room temperature, or even cold, though they're better fresh. They will keep in the refrigerator for 2 days.

SEE HOW-TO ON FOLLOWING PAGES

1 Whisk the eggs together, then fold in the chopped scallion, minced carrot, and salt.

2 Heat the pan over low or medium-low heat—err on the side of lower on your first attempt, because you don't want the eggs to heavily brown.

3 Lightly grease the pan with just a little oil, spreading it around evenly with a paper towel and making sure to blot up excess oil.

4 Pour in the egg mixture—it's easiest to use a ¼-cup (60 ml) measuring cup. Make sure the eggs cover the bottom of the pan evenly.

5 Within a minute or so the eggs will just be set: Look for the edges of the omelet to turn pale yellow and slightly curl.

6 Work quickly to lay down a sheet of seaweed, if you're using it. (The roasted seaweed sheets should be cut to fit the pan, if necessary.)

CONTINUES

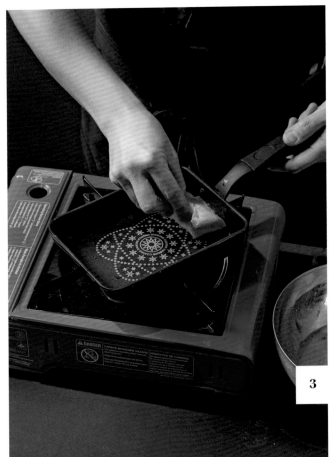

7

8

10

11

7 Use a flexible spatula to start rolling the omelet up as tightly as you can from one side.

8 Push the rolled omelet all the way to one side, then pour another ¼ cup (60 ml) of beaten egg into the pan.

9 Swirl the egg so it covers the bottom of the pan, making sure it touches the already cooked omelet. You want them to meld together into one big omelet.

10 When the second part of the omelet is just cooked, lay down another sheet of roasted seaweed.

11 Roll the first omelet into the second one so you end up with one fat roll of omelet.

12 Use your spatula to move the omelet to one side, pressing it against the side into a slightly rectangular shape.

13 Remove the roll to the cutting board and cut it into fat slices.

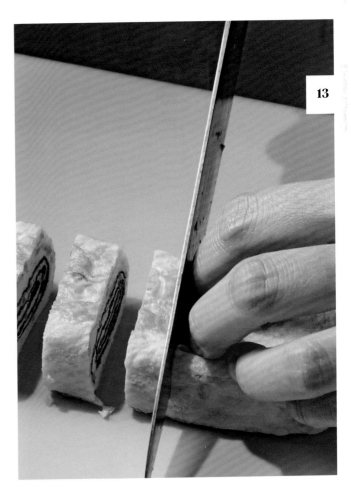

YACHAE TWIGIM

VEGETABLE FRITTERS

These lacy fritters are one of the most popular street snacks in Korea, fried to order and dunked, like most fried things, in a salty-sweet dipping sauce. You can use almost any vegetables for these, as long as they have a low water content. One secret to their crispness and crunch is that you toss the vegetables in a bit of flour and potato starch, which makes it easier to coat them in batter, otherwise it tends to slip off. Another is that when you drop them in the pot to fry, keep them slightly messy and lacy, so you end up with extra cracks and crevices. It also helps to place them on a cooling rack once they're fried, rather than paper towels, so they don't get soggy.

Serves 6 to 8

Vegetable oil,
  for frying

2 cups (240 g)
  julienned carrots

2 cups (145 g)
  julienned sweet
  potatoes

1 cup (240 g)
  julienned
  zucchini

½ cup (145 g)
  julienned
  potatoes

½ cup (30 g)
  julienned
  perilla leaves
  or scallions cut
  into 2-inch
  (5 cm) pieces

1 cup (120 g) plus
  2 tablespoons
  all-purpose flour

1 cup (150 g) plus
  2 tablespoons
  potato starch

1 teaspoon kosher
  salt, plus extra
  for garnish

1 to 3 cups
  (240 to 700 ml)
  cold seltzer

Haemul Pajeon
  dipping sauce
  (page 44)

1   Fill a skillet about halfway with oil. Heat the oil over medium-high heat to 350°F (175°C), or until it is lightly shimmering.

2   While the oil heats, mix together the carrots, sweet potatoes, zucchini, potatoes, and perilla leaves in a large mixing bowl. Add 2 tablespoons of the flour and 2 tablespoons of the potato starch and toss the vegetables until they are coated with the flour and starch.

3   In another large mixing bowl, combine the remaining flour and starch, the salt, and the seltzer until it reaches the consistency of a loose crepe batter, adding more seltzer as needed.

4   Transfer the floured vegetables to the bowl of batter and stir to coat them well.

5   Use two large spoons to drop about ⅓ cup (75 ml) of the vegetables and batter slowly into the hot oil, watching for spatters. (The fritter should be lacy and slightly uneven around the edges, like a bird's nest.) Work in batches to fry several fritters at a time, leaving plenty of space between them in the pan. Cook the fritters on one side for 2 to 3 minutes, or until the edges are golden brown, then flip and cook them until they are crispy, about 2 minutes more.

6   Use a slotted spoon to strain them out of the oil and transfer them to a wire cooling rack. Immediately sprinkle them with salt.

7   Serve hot or at room temperature with the dipping sauce.

Twigim

(Crispy Fried)

BUGAK
CRISPY FRIED SEAWEED CHIPS

Salty and crunchy, this is a
fantastic *banchan* or *anju*,
the Korean term for food you
consume while you're drinking
alcohol. (Just put these crisp
shards out with roasted, salted
nuts.) *Bugak* is also the perfect
partner to Yukhwe, the Korean
steak tartare on page 182. Be sure
to fry these at a slightly higher
temperature than usual.

NOTE: You can make this with any stock
you have on hand, or water. I usually
make it with quick shrimp stock made
from shrimp shells or lobster shells: Just
simmer them in a few cups of water for
about 30 minutes.

Makes about a dozen large chips

1 cup (184 g)
    leftover
    cooked rice

2 cups (480 ml)
    Master Anchovy
    Stock (page 228)
    or water
    (see Note)

6 large sheets
    roasted seaweed,
    halved

Vegetable oil,
    for frying

Sea salt

1   Preheat the oven to 120°F (49°C).

2   Combine the rice and the stock or
    water in a pot and bring it to a boil over
    medium-high heat. Let it cook for 5
    minutes, then stir it until it is a thick but
    spreadable paste.

3   Let the rice paste cool, then brush it on
    each piece of roasted seaweed. Thin with
    water if necessary to spread evenly.

4   Put the seaweed pieces on a rack set in a
    baking sheet, and bake them for 6 to 10
    hours, or until the topping is completely
    dried. (This stage is shown in the Korean
    Kitchen, page 13.)

5   Fill a Dutch oven or heavy-bottomed pot
    about halfway with oil, then heat it until
    right before it really begins to shimmer,
    about 400°F (205°C). Line a baking sheet
    with paper towels.

6   Fry the seaweed pieces 1 or 2 at a time
    just until the rice puffs up and the sheets
    become crunchy, about 2 to 3 minutes.
    Remove the bugak from the oil with
    a slotted spoon or spider to the paper
    towels and immediately season them
    with salt. When the bugak are cool, break
    them up into a few large, irregular chips.

7   Serve immediately or keep for 2 to 3 days
    in an airtight container.

AUH-MUK BOKKEUM

SAUTÉED FISH CAKES WITH VEGETABLES

When I was very young and still living in Korea, my grandmother would take me to the market every day to shop for dinner: fresh fish, fresh produce, fresh everything. I have strong memories of the fresh fish cakes made there, called *auh-muk*. They're made of cooked white fish, like pollack, mixed with fillers, like potato starch, seasoned with spices, salt, and sugar, and then formed and fried into these super-tasty processed sheets that you can cut into noodle shapes and simmer into stew or add to a sauté. (Now they're sold frozen, though everyone still calls them "market fish cakes.") My grandmother always pan-fried them into a quick *banchan* with chiles and onions. This is best hot off the pan, but you can keep it for a day or two. Despite the deliciousness, you don't want to eat a lot of these: They put a lot of MSG in these little cakes—it's what makes them taste so darn good!

NOTE: Look for flat sheets of fried fish cakes in the frozen section of a Korean supermarket. You can quickly defrost them, still wrapped in their packaging, in a bowl of water.

Serves 4

2 tablespoons soy sauce

1 tablespoon mirin

2 teaspoons minced garlic

1 tablespoon sesame oil

½ teaspoon kosher salt

⅛ teaspoon freshly ground black pepper

2 tablespoons grapeseed or olive oil

½ yellow onion, thinly sliced

1 Korean green chile, seeded and cut into ½-inch (12 mm) strips on the bias

1 Korean red chile, seeded and cut into ½-inch (12 mm) strips on the bias

½ pound (225 g) fish cakes (see Note), cut into 2 by 1-inch (5 by 2.5 cm) strips

1   In a small mixing bowl, whisk together the soy sauce, mirin, garlic, sesame oil, salt, black pepper, and 2 tablespoons water. Set aside.

2   In a skillet, heat the grapeseed oil over medium-high heat. Add the onion, chiles, and fish cakes and cook them, stirring constantly, for 2 to 3 minutes.

3   Reduce the heat and add the soy sauce mixture to the pan. Let the fish cakes cook, stirring often, until the liquid evaporates and the fish cakes are golden brown.

4   This is best served while still hot, but you can serve it at room temperature, or even chilled. It will keep in the refrigerator for about 1 to 2 days.

Bokkeum

(Stir-Fried)

BUH-SUT BOKKEUM

MUSHROOM STIR-FRY

This quick stir-fry serves as a neutral *banchan* to offset anything very spicy or salty. You can get as exotic as you want with the variety of mushrooms and substitute any varieties you choose, like king oysters or porcini.

Serves 2 to 4

2 tablespoons
canola oil

10 ounces (280 g)
cremini mushrooms,
thick stems
trimmed, sliced
⅛ inch (3 mm)
thick

6 ounces (170 g)
shiitake mushroom
caps, sliced
¼ inch (6 mm)
thick

1 tablespoon thinly
sliced scallion,
whites only

1 tablespoon
minced garlic

1 large Korean
green chile or
jalapeño, seeded
and thinly sliced

¼ teaspoon
kosher salt

2 teaspoons
sesame oil

3 teaspoons
soy sauce

¼ cup (60 ml)
Master Anchovy
Stock (page 228)
or water

1 teaspoon rice
wine vinegar

1 teaspoon shilgochu
(Korean chile
threads), for
garnish

1   In a wok or a large skillet, heat 1 tablespoon of the canola oil over high heat. Add the mushrooms and cook, stirring occasionally, for about 5 minutes, or until any liquid they exude starts to evaporate and the mushrooms are nicely browned.

2   Add another tablespoon of canola oil. Add the scallion, garlic, chile, and salt and cook for another minute.

3   Add the sesame oil, soy sauce, and stock. Using a spatula or wooden spoon, scrape any collected bits from the bottom of the pan.

4   Remove the pan from the heat and stir in the rice wine vinegar.

5   Serve hot or at room temperature, garnished with the chile threads. It will keep in the refrigerator for 2 to 3 days.

OJINGO BOKKEUM
FRESH SQUID STIR-FRY

I am a big fan of squid for so many reasons: It's sustainable, it's low in fat (so long as you don't bread and deep-fry it), and it's a good source of protein. But most importantly, it's always under five dollars a pound! It's often the only affordable item when I stand there cringing at the prices at the fish market. And it's also delicious—this squid stir-fry with carrots, chiles, and onion packs a flavor punch like no other dish, especially considering how little time it takes to make. Once you prep everything, the cooking time is less than ten minutes. I often serve this with rice or noodles as a real meal.

Serves 4 to 6

FOR THE SAUCE

- 2 tablespoons gochujang
- 1 tablespoon gochugaru
- 4½ teaspoons granulated sugar
- 1 tablespoon soy sauce
- 1 tablespoon minced garlic
- 1 tablespoon toasted sesame seeds
- 2 teaspoons sesame oil

FOR THE SQUID

- 2 tablespoons grapeseed or olive oil
- ½ medium white onion, cut lengthwise into thick slices
- 1 small carrot, thinly sliced on the bias
- 1 Korean green chile or jalapeño, thinly sliced
- 3 scallions, white parts thinly sliced, green parts cut into 2-inch (5 cm) pieces
- 2 pounds (910 g) cleaned squid, bodies cut into ¼-inch (6 mm) rings (see Note, page 150)

1   Make the sauce: Combine the gochujang, gochugaru, sugar, soy sauce, garlic, sesame seeds, and sesame oil in a small bowl and set it aside.

2   Make the squid: In a wok or a large skillet, heat 1 tablespoon of the oil over high heat. Add the onion, carrot, chile, and scallions and cook for 3 to 4 minutes, stirring often, until the vegetables begin to soften and char. Remove them from the pan to a bowl and set aside.

3   Add the remaining tablespoon of oil to the pan, and when it begins to smoke, add the squid. Cook it, stirring constantly, for 1 minute, then add the sauce and the cooked vegetables. Toss it all together and cook, stirring constantly, for another 2 to 3 minutes, or until the squid is cooked through and everything is coated in the sauce.

4   Taste the dish, and adjust the seasoning with more soy sauce, sugar, or gochujang if desired, then serve immediately.

MYULCHI BOKKEUM

CANDIED ANCHOVIES WITH PEANUTS

You might be surprised to find that this is a crowd-pleaser of a *banchan*! Even kids love these sweet, salty, crispy little fish. (And for adults, it makes a great *anju*, or drinking snack.) You can also try adding dried goji berries, sunflower seeds, and other goodies to make an addictive Korean trail mix. (If you go hiking with Chef Michael Stokes of Insa, he just might have a bag of these to share with you.)

NOTE: Asian or Korean supermarkets usually stock small bags of dried anchovies in multiple sizes. For this dish you want tiny, silvery, toothpick-wide baby fish or just slightly bigger.

Serves 8 to 10

½ pound (225 g) dried baby anchovies (see Note)

¼ cup (60 ml) olive oil

½ cup (65 g) roasted peanuts

1 tablespoon minced garlic

¼ cup (60 ml) packed brown sugar

3 tablespoons soy sauce

¼ cup (15 g) thinly sliced scallion

1 tablespoon toasted sesame seeds

1   Heat a large skillet over medium heat, then toast the anchovies in the dry pan for about a minute. Add the oil and cook the anchovies, stirring occasionally, for another minute.

2   Add the peanuts, garlic, sugar, and soy sauce.

3   Reduce the heat to medium-low and cook for another few minutes, stirring often, until the sugar, garlic, and soy sauce are well incorporated.

4   Stir in the scallion, turn off the heat, and add the sesame seeds. Toss everything until well combined.

5   Let the dish cool to room temperature, then serve, or store for up to a week in an airtight container.

MAE-UN MYULCHI BOKKEUM

SPICY ANCHOVY STIR-FRY

Another classic *banchan*, one
that keeps really well and is salty,
sweet, and so spicy. This one
is designed to be a meal flavor
booster that can last in your
refrigerator for weeks.

---

3 tablespoons
  gochujang

1 tablespoon
  gochugaru

1 tablespoon
  soy sauce

1 tablespoon mirin

1 tablespoon
  minced garlic

2 teaspoon packed
  brown sugar

2 tablespoons
  brown rice syrup

3 tablespoons olive
  oil

½ pound (about
  4 cups/225 g)
  dried anchovies

2 scallions,
  thinly sliced

1 tablespoon
  toasted sesame
  seeds

1 In a mixing bowl, whisk together the
   gochujang, gochugaru, soy sauce, mirin,
   garlic, brown sugar, and rice syrup.

2 In a large skillet or medium saucepan,
   heat the olive oil over medium heat.
   Add the anchovies and cook, stirring
   constantly, for about 2 minutes or until
   they are all well toasted.

3 Reduce the heat to medium-low, then add
   the gochujang-soy mixture to the pot. Let
   the anchovies cook, stirring often, for
   about 2 to 3 minutes, or until all of them
   are coated. Be careful not to let them
   burn; lower the heat if necessary.

4 Transfer the anchovies to a serving bowl,
   then add the scallions and sesame seeds
   and toss to mix. This can be stored in the
   refrigerator for about 2 weeks.

BUTCHU OI MUCHIM

MARINATED CUCUMBERS

Muchim

(Tossed)

This is the quickest little salad you could possibly put together, a fresh and crisp mix of cucumbers, Chinese garlic chives we call *butchu*, and sweet white onion. It's meant to be eaten fresh—after three to four days the cucumbers start to pickle and lose their crunch. Just be sure to remove some if not all of the seeds and seed membrane from the center of the cucumber, because they can make this *banchan* bitter and watery.

```
If you're going to
make banchan a lot,
you really need a
good-size stainless-
steel mixing bowl.
It makes hand-tossing
muchim, namul banchan,
or any dish where
you mix things up
much easier. I have
my favorite well-worn
mixing bowl and so
should you.
```

Serves 4 to 6

```
1½ pounds (680 g)
    Korean, English
    hothouse, or
    Persian cucumbers

¼ pound (115 g,
    or about 1 large
    bunch) Chinese
    garlic chives,
    cut into 1½-inch
    (4 cm) pieces

1 cup (100 g)
    thinly sliced
    sweet white onion

2 tablespoons
    gochugaru

2 tablespoons rice
    wine vinegar

2 teaspoons packed
    brown sugar

1 tablespoon
    sesame oil

1 tablespoon toasted
    sesame seeds

1½ teaspoons
    kosher salt
```

1 Cut the cucumbers into 2-inch (5 cm) pieces, then cut each of those pieces in half lengthwise. Remove most of the seeds from each piece.

2 Cut each piece into thirds lengthwise, so you have three 2-inch (5 cm) sticks.

3 Place the cucumbers in a large mixing bowl, then add the garlic chives, onion, gochugaru, rice wine vinegar, brown sugar, sesame oil, sesame seeds, and salt.

4 Mix everything together well with your hands, then pack it into a nonreactive storage container, such as glass or plastic.

5 You can eat this right away, but it tastes better if left to sit at room temperature for 15 minutes. This will last 3 to 4 days in the refrigerator.

OIJJANGACHI MUCHIM

PICKLED CUCUMBER SALAD

This is our version of pickled cucumber salad. *Oi* means "cucumber," and *jangachi* means "pickled vegetables." The cucumbers are dressed with sesame oil, chile flakes, scallions, and sesame seeds after they have been pickled for two weeks. Steps one through five are simply making plain cucumber pickles: You could use them in the Miyeok Oi Muchim salad on page 76 or any way you like.

NOTE: As with most *muchim*-style *ban-chan*, use your hands to toss everything together to make sure it is well seasoned. Since this recipe calls for chile flakes, consider wearing gloves to protect yourself from burns.

Serves 4 to 6

1 pound (455 g) whole Kirby or small Persian cucumbers

¼ cup (60 g) kosher salt

½ cup (120 ml) rice wine vinegar

1 tablespoon sesame oil

½ teaspoon granulated sugar

1 teaspoon sesame seeds

2 teaspoons gochugaru

1 teaspoon minced garlic

1 scallion, halved lengthwise and thinly sliced

1   Put the cucumbers in a heat-proof, nonreactive mixing bowl or a heat-proof canning jar or plastic storage container.

2   In a small saucepan, bring the salt, rice wine vinegar, and 2 cups (480 ml) water to a boil, then pour the mixture over the cucumbers. Let them sit, covered, at room temperature for 24 hours.

3   Pour the brine from the cucumbers into a small saucepan and bring it to a boil, then pour it back over the cucumbers.

4   Let cool to room temperature, then cover and refrigerate for 2 weeks, or until the cucumbers are fully soft and shriveled.

5   Slice the cucumbers into ¼-inch (6 mm) slices and place them in a mixing bowl.

6   Dress with the sesame oil, sugar, sesame seeds, gochugaru, garlic, and scallion, tossing the cucumbers with your hands (see Note) until everything is well mixed.

7   Serve cold or at room temperature. It keeps for about 2 weeks in the refrigerator.

FENNEL MUCHIM

FENNEL SALAD

Crunchy, tart, spicy, and delicious, this *muchim* is best made with large bulbs of fennel, because you usually lose a few layers of outer leaves to bruising. I have never seen fennel used in Korea, but when I get an abundance of American seasonal vegetables, I find I have great success in transforming it to work with Korean flavors. If your bulbs come with the greens attached, feel free to add a few of the very tender tips to this muchim, too.

```
With any recipe where
I make a gochujang-
based sauce, I always
measure the sesame
oil first, so the
gochujang paste just
glides off the spoon.
```

Serves 6 to 8

```
2 pounds (910 g)
  fennel bulbs

Kosher salt

2 tablespoons
  sesame oil

1/4 cup (60 ml)
  gochujang

2 1/2 teaspoons
  gochugaru

1 tablespoon
  toasted sesame
  seeds

3 tablespoons rice
  wine vinegar

1 teaspoon
  minced garlic

1 teaspoon
  minced peeled
  fresh ginger

2 tablespoons honey
```

1   Peel and discard any thick or bruised outer leaves from the fennel bulbs. Quarter the bulbs, cut out the cores, and then thinly slice each quarter into 1/4-inch (6 mm) slices. Set them aside.

2   Bring 2 gallons (7.5 L) water to a boil in a large pot and add 1/3 cup (80 g) salt. While it comes to a boil, prepare a large mixing bowl with 2 quarts (2 L) cold water and 1 quart (960 ml) ice cubes. Stir in 1/4 cup (60 g) salt.

3   Blanch the fennel bulb slices in the boiling water for 2 minutes, then remove them and plunge them immediately into the ice water. (Keep the water at a boil.) Use your hands to toss the fennel slices in the cold water, making sure they are chilled as fast as possible. Working quickly so they don't get waterlogged, remove the fennel from the water and transfer them to a colander set into a mixing bowl.

4   In a large mixing bowl, combine the sesame oil, gochujang, gochugaru, sesame seeds, rice wine vinegar, garlic, ginger, and honey.

5   Add the sliced fennel and mix everything together with your hands until the fennel is well coated with the sauce.

6   Place the fennel muchim in a nonreactive storage container.

7   You can eat this right away, but it tastes better if left to sit at room temperature for 15 minutes. It will last 3 to 4 days in the refrigerator.

MIYEOK OI MUCHIM

SEAWEED, CUCUMBER, AND CHARRED LEEK SALAD

A refreshing salad for the summer or any time cucumbers are in season. This is great with Haemul Pajeon, the seafood and scallion pancakes on page 44, or as a foil to anything fried.

Serves 4 to 6

½ ounce (14 g) dried wakame or miyeok seaweed (see Miyeok Guk, page 198)

1 small leek or 3 scallions

½ pound (225 g) Kirby or Persian cucumbers, sliced ¼ inch (6 mm) thick (or use pickled cucumbers from Oijjangachi Muchim, page 72)

1 to 2 teaspoons kosher salt

1 teaspoon minced garlic

2 tablespoons soy sauce

¼ cup (60 ml) apple cider vinegar

2 tablespoons toasted sesame seeds

1 Soak the seaweed in a bowl of hot water for about 30 minutes, then squeeze out the water and let the seaweed drain in a colander in the sink.

2 Heat a skillet over medium-high heat, then cook the leek in the dry pan until it is charred on all sides. Let cool and roughly chop.

3 Put the seaweed and the leek in a mixing bowl, then add the cucumbers or cucumber pickles, salt, garlic, soy sauce, vinegar, and sesame seeds.

4 Mix everything together with your hands until it is well incorporated, then serve at room temperature. You can also refrigerate for 2 to 3 days.

OJiNGOCHAE MUCHIM

SPICY DRIED SQUID

The *New York Times* called this *banchan* "a time release of flavor." It hits all the right notes: sweet, spicy, salty, and a little chewy.

NOTE: If the dried squid are fresh, you should be able to easily cut them into pieces. If they are very dried out and coarse, try steaming them for 5 minutes. It is best to wear disposable plastic gloves when massaging the marinade into the dried squid.

Serves 8 to 10

1 pound (455 g)
  dried squid
  (see Note)

½ cup (120 ml)
  gochujang

1 tablespoon
  minced garlic

⅓ cup (75 ml)
  grapeseed or
  olive oil

1 tablespoon
  soy sauce

1 tablespoon
  sesame oil

2 tablespoons honey
  or rice syrup

1 tablespoon packed
  brown sugar

Gochugaru, for
  garnish

Toasted sesame
  seeds, for
  garnish

1 Cut the dried squid into bite-size pieces with kitchen shears into a mixing bowl (see Note).

2 Add the gochujang, garlic, grapeseed oil, soy sauce, sesame oil, honey, and brown sugar to a small saucepan over medium heat. Cook, stirring often, until the sugar melts and the ingredients are well incorporated, a minute or two. Add the sauce to the mixing bowl with the squid.

3 Toss everything together, then massage the marinade into the squid with your hands (see Note).

4 Transfer the dried squid to a serving bowl and sprinkle it with gochugaru and sesame seeds. This will keep covered in the refrigerator for several weeks.

NOKDU MUK

MUNG BEAN STARCH JELLY

Though mild in flavor, these beautiful, glassy delicacies are so much fun to make and serve. (The real trick is picking them up with chopsticks.) The kimchi sauce I serve with them is also fantastic tossed with just about any noodle or vegetable. This is really best fresh, as it tends to take on a milky color and lose its springiness over time.

NOTE: You'll find mung bean starch at Korean markets or stores with alternative flours for the gluten-free.

Serves 6 to 8

FOR THE MUNG BEAN JELLY

½ cup (95 g) mung bean starch (see Note)

1 teaspoon salt

FOR THE KIMCHI SAUCE

½ cup (75 g) diced Baechu Kimchi (page 102)

2 tablespoons soy sauce

1 teaspoon packed brown sugar

2 scallions, sliced thin

1 teaspoon minced garlic

2 tablespoons sesame oil

1 tablespoon toasted sesame seeds

1 small sheet roasted seaweed, crushed

1 Make the mung bean jelly: In a heavy-bottomed pot, combine the mung bean starch with 3½ cups (840 ml) cold water.

2 Bring the mixture to a low boil over medium to medium-high heat. Stirring constantly, let the mixture cook for 7 minutes.

3 Add the salt and let cook for 2 minutes more.

4 Lower the heat to a simmer and let cook for about 2 to 3 minutes more, or until it looks like jelly and is bubbly and translucent.

5 Transfer the jelly to a glass or ceramic pan that is 5 by 7 inches (12 by 17 cm) wide and 3 to 4 inches (7.5 to 10 cm) deep, preferably with a lid.

6 Let the jelly cool, uncovered, in the pan for 1 hour, then cover it and refrigerate for at least 3 hours and preferably overnight, or until the jelly is firm and solid.

7 Cut the jelly into bite-size pieces and place them in a serving bowl.

8 Make the kimchi sauce: In a small bowl, combine the kimchi, soy sauce, sugar, scallions, garlic, sesame oil, and sesame seeds until the sugar has dissolved.

9 Toss the mung bean jelly with the dressing, then garnish with the crushed seaweed and serve immediately.

SANGCHU MUCHIM

GRILLED ESCAROLE MUCHIM

Not so traditional, but absolutely delicious. Smoky charred scallions and bitter escarole are just beautiful with this sweet, garlicky sesame dressing. This dish can be made with other hearty lettuces or greens like kale.

Serves 6 to 8

1½ pounds (680 g) escarole (about 2 heads)

1 bunch scallions, roots trimmed

Grapeseed or olive oil, for greasing

Kosher salt

2 tablespoons sesame oil

2 tablespoons soy sauce

1 teaspoon minced garlic

1 teaspoon granulated sugar

2 teaspoons fish sauce

1 tablespoon toasted sesame seeds

1   Heat a large cast-iron skillet or grill pan over medium-high heat until smoking hot.

2   Rub the escarole and scallions all over with the grapeseed oil and lightly salt them. Cook the escarole on the skillet or grill pan, flipping once or twice, until nicely charred, then set aside on a cutting board. Do the same with the scallion stalks. Let cool completely.

3   Cut the cooled escarole and scallions into 1-inch (2.5 cm) pieces and place them in a mixing bowl.

4   Add the sesame oil, soy sauce, garlic, sugar, fish sauce, and sesame seeds and toss until everything is coated with the seasoning. Taste for seasoning and add salt as necessary.

5   Serve at room temperature or chilled. It keeps for about 2 to 3 days in the refrigerator.

GU OON HOBAK MUCHIM

CHARRED SUMMER SQUASH SALAD

I love this jazzed-up version of grilled summer squash. You can easily cut this recipe in half, or use just yellow crooknecks or zucchini instead of both.

Serves 8 to 10

1 pound (455 g)
  yellow crookneck
  squash

1 pound (455 g)
  zucchini

2 tablespoons
  grapeseed oil

2 tablespoons
  sesame oil

3 tablespoons
  gochujang

1½ teaspoons
  gochugaru

2 tablespoons
  toasted
  sesame seeds

3 tablespoons rice
  wine vinegar

1 teaspoon
  minced garlic

1 teaspoon
  minced peeled
  fresh ginger

1 tablespoon honey
  (optional)

½ cup (23 g)
  minced scallions

Kosher salt

1   Slice the squash and zucchini into ½-inch (12 mm) rounds and place them in a large mixing bowl. Add the grapeseed oil, tossing the vegetables until all are coated.

2   Heat a grill pan, cast-iron skillet, or grill over medium-high heat. Grill the squash slices, flipping them once or twice, until they are slightly tender and browned or charred on both sides, about 5 minutes. Remove them from the pan or grill to cool in a colander set over a bowl or the sink, letting any liquid drain off.

3   Wipe out the mixing bowl and add the sesame oil, gochujang, gochugaru, sesame seeds, rice wine vinegar, garlic, ginger, and honey, if using, whisking until they are mixed together.

4   Add the cooled, drained squash and toss the slices with your hands until everything is well coated with the sauce.

5   Add the scallions and toss again until everything is mixed together, adding salt to taste. Serve at room temperature or cold. It will last in the fridge for 2 to 3 days.

MOO SAENGCHAE

QUICK-PICKLED RADISH

This is served both as *banchan* and as a traditional topping for things like the cold noodle dish Bibim Naeng Myeon on page 242. It's also great with any Korean BBQ: A bit of this pickle in a *ssam* (lettuce wrap) with grilled meats is delicious! As with Baechu Kimchi, the key step is salting the radish slices before you toss them with other ingredients, until they are very soft, or what Koreans call *juginda*, "to kill."

Makes 1 quart (945 ml)

1½ pounds (680 g)
   moo radish

1 tablespoon
   kosher salt

1 teaspoon
   minced garlic

¼ cup (60 ml) rice
   wine vinegar

1 tablespoon
   gochugaru

1 scallion, halved
   lengthwise and
   thinly sliced

1 teaspoon
   granulated sugar

1   Cut the radish lengthwise into quarters, then slice each quarter paper thin using a mandoline, chef's knife, or food processor fitted with the slicing blade.

2   Transfer the radish slices to a mixing bowl and sprinkle with the salt. Use your hands to toss the radish slices in the salt, separating them where necessary, until every piece is coated. Let them sit for 15 minutes.

3   Transfer the slices to a colander and, working over the sink, squeeze out all the water from the radishes with your hands.

4   Wipe out the mixing bowl and combine the drained radishes, garlic, rice wine vinegar, gochugaru, scallion, and sugar, and mix with your hands until everything is well coated.

5   Let the radishes sit for 1 hour, then serve at room temperature or keep refrigerated for up to 1 week.

MOO MALLENG E MUCHIM

PICKLED DRIED RADISH

This is another *banchan* you should think of as a technique, rather than a recipe: This can be made with any dried and reconstituted vegetable, of which there are many in Asian markets. Koreans dry excess vegetables that aren't consumed within a season to preserve for later. This is the most popular dried vegetable next to dried fern bracken. Most, like these dried sliced radishes, are sold in plastic packages.

Serves 8 to 10

4 cups (about
   7 ounces/200 g)
   dried, sliced
   radish

2 tablespoons
   soy sauce

4 cups (960 ml)
   lukewarm water

2 tablespoons
   minced garlic

⅓ cup (80 ml)
   gochugaru

2 tablespoons
   sesame oil

2 tablespoons
   fish sauce

¼ cup (60 ml) brown
   rice syrup

2 teaspoons toasted
   sesame seeds

1 tablespoon
   shilgochu (Korean
   chile threads)

2 scallions,
   thinly sliced

1   Place the dried radishes and soy sauce in a large mixing bowl and add the water. Let the radishes soak for 10 minutes.

2   Rinse the dried radishes well in a colander under plenty of running water and then let them drain in the sink or over a bowl until completely dry.

3   In a large mixing bowl, combine the garlic, gochugaru, sesame oil, fish sauce, rice syrup, sesame seeds, chile threads, and scallions. Fold in the radishes and mix everything by hand until the radishes are well coated.

4   Serve at room temperature or chilled. It keeps in the refrigerator for up to 3 weeks.

KONG NAMUL

SOYBEAN SPROUT SALAD

Namul

(Seasoned

Greens)

This *namul*, made with fresh soybean sprouts, is one of my favorites. The crisp texture and crunch provide balance to all the other hot and salty things on the table. As an extra bonus, the liquid that accumulates at the bottom of the dish is delicious; be sure to spoon it over your rice. Leftovers can go into bibimbop for lunch the next day. If you can't find soybean sprouts, you can also make this with mung bean sprouts.

Serves 4 to 6

12 ounces (340 g) soybean sprouts

1½ teaspoons kosher salt

2 tablespoons sesame oil

1 teaspoon minced garlic

1 teaspoon gochugaru

2½ teaspoons fish sauce (optional)

2 tablespoons finely sliced scallion

¼ teaspoon freshly ground black pepper

1   Put the sprouts in a medium saucepan and cover with water. Add 1 teaspoon of the salt, bring the water to a boil, and let the sprouts cook at a low boil for 5 minutes.

2   Drain the sprouts and let them cool completely.

3   In a mixing bowl, toss the cooled sprouts with the sesame oil, garlic, gochugaru, fish sauce, if using, scallion, black pepper and remaining ½ teaspoon salt. Mix until everything is well incorporated and the sprouts are fully coated. Feel free to add more gochugaru for extra kick or more salt if desired.

4   Serve at room temperature. It will last for 2 to 3 days in the refrigerator.

GEUN-DAE NAMUL

SWISS CHARD NAMUL

For this classic *namul*, I use various green leafy vegetables that we get from our local farmer and friend Patty Gentry of Early Girl Farms. You can easily steam the greens instead of sautéing them in a pan—just be sure to get rid of excess water by squeezing it out with your hands.

NOTE: Perilla oil, made from the seeds of the perilla plant, has a similar flavor and aroma to sesame oil but a little more brightness. White soy sauce has a golden color and a different flavor than regular soy sauce, because it is usually brewed with more wheat or other grains, so you can't sub in dark soy sauce here. Both are easily found at Korean or Asian markets.

Serves 2 to 4

1 bunch (12 to 16 ounces/340 to 455 g) green Swiss chard

1 tablespoon grapeseed or olive oil

1 tablespoon perilla oil or sesame oil (see Note)

1 tablespoon minced garlic

1 tablespoon white soy sauce (see Note)

2 teaspoons fish sauce (optional)

1 Roughly chop the chard leaves and thinly slice the stems, keeping them separate.

2 In a large skillet or wok, heat the grapeseed oil over medium-high heat. Add the Swiss chard stems first and let them cook, stirring frequently, for 3 minutes.

3 Add the chard leaves, stirring constantly, and as soon as they shrink down (about a minute), add the perilla oil, garlic, soy sauce, and fish sauce, if using. Continue to cook until the chard is cooked through, about 3 to 4 minutes.

4 Serve hot or at room temperature. It will keep in the refrigerator for 2 days.

GOSARI NAMUL

BRACKEN SALAD

Gosari is dried Korean fern, also known as bracken. It is so dried that it takes an overnight soak to bring it back to life, but the hours are worth it: Gosari is earthy and delicious, packed with protein, and almost beefy in texture. This *banchan* will keep for up to a week, and it is *so* good with the bibimbop sauce from page 246 and hot rice for an easy lunch! For some reason this banchan is always at formal gatherings, perhaps because it's an old dish originally made from foraged plants.

Serves 6 to 8

2 ounces (55 g)
    dried Korean
    bracken

2 tablespoons
    grapeseed or
    olive oil

3 tablespoons
    soy sauce

2 tablespoons
    diced scallion

2 tablespoons
    minced garlic

1 tablespoon
    sesame oil

1 tablespoon
    toasted sesame
    seeds

1   Cover the bracken with plenty of water in a large pot and let sit at room temperature overnight.

2   Drain the bracken and use kitchen shears to roughly cut it into 2-inch (5 cm) pieces. Cover the bracken with cold water, place the pot over high heat, and bring it to a boil.

3   Lower the heat so that the bracken cooks at a simmer until it is soft, about 30 minutes to 1 hour. Drain and rinse the bracken.

4   In a skillet, heat the oil over medium-high heat and add the drained bracken. Let it cook, stirring occasionally, for 2 minutes.

5   Stir in the soy sauce, scallion, and garlic, and cook for another 2 minutes. If the pan is very dry, add 1 or 2 tablespoons water.

6   Remove the pan from the heat and stir in the sesame oil and sesame seeds.

7   Let this sit at room temperature for 15 minutes before serving; you can also serve it chilled. It will last 3 to 4 days in the refrigerator.

MULNAENG-E NAMUL
WATERCRESS NAMUL

This is the quintessential *namul* recipe. Most Koreans use spinach, but I like the flavor and slight bite of watercress. You can use whichever greens look fresh at the market.

Serves 2 to 4

1 pound (455 g)
  watercress or
  spinach, tough
  stems removed

1 tablespoon
  kosher salt

1 tablespoon
  soy sauce

Fish sauce
  (optional)

1 tablespoon
  sesame oil

2 teaspoons
  minced garlic

2 scallions,
  thinly sliced

1 teaspoon toasted
  sesame seeds

Freshly ground
  black pepper

1 Bring a pot of lightly salted water to a boil and prepare a bowl of lightly salted ice water. Blanch the watercress in the boiling water for 45 seconds, then immediately remove it to the ice water. Move the greens around with your clean hands until cooled. Drain them immediately and squeeze all the water out with your hands.

2 Roughly chop the watercress and transfer it to a mixing bowl. Add the soy sauce, fish sauce, if using, sesame oil, garlic, scallions, sesame seeds, and black pepper to taste. (You can also add more fish sauce, soy sauce, etc., to taste.)

3 Serve at room temperature or chilled. It will keep in the refrigerator for 2 days, but it is better eaten within a day.

GAJI NAMUL
CHARRED EGGPLANT WITH WHITE SOY AND CHILES

Typically you would steam the eggplant—*gaji*—for this very traditional side dish, but I've become fond of roasting or pan-searing vegetables for *banchan* over the years. (Of course, you can also grill them outside, if you like.) Steamed eggplants tend to get waterlogged and have to be drained, losing a lot of their flavor. This way, you can really taste the eggplant, and the smoky char adds a layer of complexity.

Serves 2 to 4

1 pound (455 kg)
  Japanese eggplant

Vegetable oil

2 scallions, halved
  lengthwise and
  then thinly
  sliced (see
  page 14)

2 teaspoons
  minced garlic

2 teaspoons toasted
  sesame seeds

2 teaspoons white
  soy sauce (see
  Note, page 92)

1 teaspoon
  fish sauce

2 teaspoons
  sesame oil

1 tablespoon thinly
  sliced Holland
  chile, seeds
  removed

1   Cut the eggplant into 2-inch (5 cm) pieces, then cut those in half lengthwise. (Leave the skin on.)

2   Lightly coat a griddle or cast-iron skillet with vegetable oil, then heat the pan over high heat.

3   Place the eggplant pieces cut side down on the griddle or skillet—working in batches if you need to—and let them cook undisturbed until the cut side is charred, about 2 minutes. Watch your heat—you want the eggplants to char, but you don't want them to burn.

4   Flip the eggplant pieces over and let the other side brown slightly, about a minute, and then lower the heat slightly and let them cook until they are just tender and cooked through, another 2 minutes. (They're done when they feel soft if you squeeze them gently with a pair of tongs.)

5   Remove the eggplant pieces to a mixing bowl and let them cool until you can handle them with your fingers. Shred each piece lengthwise into 2 to 3 strips each.

6   Add the scallions, garlic, sesame seeds, soy sauce, fish sauce, sesame oil, and chiles to the bowl, then mix everything together well with your hands. Adjust seasoning to taste.

7   Serve at room temperature or cold. It lasts for about 2 to 3 days in the refrigerator.

GAMJACHAE BANCHAN

SHREDDED POTATO SALAD

There are so many ways to serve potatoes, and this one is unique in flavor and texture. The trick with this recipe is to rinse the potatoes well before and after you cook them to remove extra starch and keep the potatoes from sticking together. (If you can steam them, they'll be even better.) You want to eat this dish the day it is made.

Serves 4 to 6

1 tablespoon
   olive oil

1 medium white
   onion, thinly
   sliced

1 pound (455 g)
   large Yukon gold
   potatoes, peeled

2 teaspoons
   kosher salt

1 tablespoon white
   soy sauce (see
   Note, page 92)

2 teaspoons
   fish sauce

2 teaspoons
   sesame oil

1 teaspoon toasted
   sesame seeds

1 teaspoon
   minced garlic

⅛ teaspoon
   freshly ground
   black pepper

2 scallions,
   thinly sliced

1   In a skillet, heat the olive oil over medium-low heat. Add the onions and cook, stirring often, until they are very soft and caramelized, about 7 minutes. Set them aside.

2   Fill a large mixing bowl with very cold water. Cut the potatoes into matchstick-size pieces (or use a mandoline to julienne them), adding them to the cold water as you go.

3   Let the cut potatoes soak in the cold water for about 5 minutes, so that they release all their starch. Rinse them a few times under cold running water, then drain.

4   Bring a large pot of water with the salt to a boil, then add the potatoes and let them cook for about 2½ minutes, or until they are just cooked through but not mushy. Immediately drain them in a sieve or colander in the sink, then rinse in cold running water until they feel cool to the touch.

5   Shake off excess water, blotting with a paper towel or two to soak up most of the water.

6   Transfer the potatoes to a mixing bowl and add the caramelized onions, soy sauce, fish sauce, sesame oil, sesame seeds, garlic, and scallions.

7   Serve hot or at room temperature the day it is made.

BAECHU KIMCHI

WHOLE NAPA CABBAGE KIMCHI

This is the master kimchi recipe, the one that non-Koreans think of when they hear the word *kimchi*—*baechu* means "cabbage." It's also known as *poggi* kimchi: Poggi means "fold," since you fold up whole cabbages and ferment them. This would traditionally have been made after the cabbage harvest as a way to preserve it. You'd pack the cabbage into clay pots, sometimes buried underground to keep them from freezing in the colder months, pulling out what you need all winter long. I've often said there is no wrong way to make kimchi, as long as your fermentation is successful, and this is my version, with fermented seafood and a paste made from sweet rice powder. Another important step is using your hands to season the cabbage, which is why it's a good idea to invest in a box of disposable plastic gloves if you plan to make this often, as the marinade can stain your hands.

NOTE: Using seafood is optional—I prefer salted shrimp (see page 12), but you can use fish sauce or raw oysters—but to me it is really necessary for the right flavor. You can make a decent vegan version by replacing the seafood or fish sauce with 1½ ounces (36 g) kombu (see page 13) and 3 tablespoons kosher salt, then putting another ½-ounce (15 g) piece of kombu at the bottom of the container. You may also choose to roughly chop the onions, red bell pepper, garlic, and ginger, put them in a food processor and pulse until incorporated, then drain them in a colander to remove the excess water.

Four great things to make with super-stinky kimchi, the kimchi that's been in your fridge for a month or longer: Kimchi Jjigae (page 206), Kimchi Jeon (page 46), Nokdu Muk (page 80), or Soondubu (page 202).

Makes 1 gallon (3.8 L)

- 2 large (3 pounds/ 1.4 kg each) napa cabbages
- 2 cups (480 g) kosher salt
- 1 tablespoon glutinous (sweet) rice flour
- 2 pounds (910 g) moo radish, julienned
- 1 onion (about 12 ounces/340 g), grated
- 1 red bell pepper, grated

- 5 tablespoons (85 g) minced garlic
- 3 tablespoons minced peeled fresh ginger
- 1½ cups (180 g) gochugaru
- 1 bunch scallions or 1 large leek, whites only, sliced ½ inch (12 mm) thick on the bias
- ½ cup (118 ml) salted shrimp, fish sauce, or freshly shucked oysters

1   Tear the cabbage into quarters lengthwise (see steps 1 to 4, pages 104-105). Fill a large bowl or pot or your sink with 8 cups (2 L) water and ¾ cup (180 g) of the salt, whisking until the salt dissolves. Dunk the cabbage quarters in the salted water, making sure all the leaves are rinsed.

2   Shake off excess water and sprinkle a good amount of salt in the folds of all the leaves, using at least ½ cup (120 g) of salt per head of cabbage.

CONTINUES

Kimchi

3   Place the salted cabbage quarters in a large bowl topped with a weight, such as a large dinner plate topped with a brick wrapped in foil or a cast-iron pot, to keep the cabbage in the juices it releases. (You could also put each quarter in a large zip-top bag.) Let them sit for at least 6 hours, or until the leaves are so flexible you can fold them in half without breaking them. (The Korean term for this is *juginda*, which roughly means "to kill.")

4   Rinse the cabbage in 3 to 4 changes of water to clean off all the extra salt, then let the pieces drain in a colander for 1 hour.

5   For the slurry, bring 1 cup (240 ml) water to a boil and whisk in the rice flour. Cook over low heat until a thick paste forms and set it aside to cool.

6   In your largest mixing bowl, combine the moo radish, onion, red bell pepper, garlic, ginger, gochugaru, scallions, and salted shrimp. Add the cooled slurry and mix together well—with your hands is really the best way.

7   Slather the marinade all over the cabbage quarters by placing a small amount on each leaf where it meets the stem, then smearing it up the leaf with your hands. Slather on more as needed until the whole cabbage is nicely covered in the marinade.

8   Make a tight bundle with each piece of cabbage, and press them into large glass containers or recycled, cleaned pickle or condiment jars, making sure there's at least 2 inches (5 cm) of space at the top for the bubbling action of the ongoing fermentation.

9   Once they are filled, keep the jars out on the counter for at least 24 hours and up to 2 days—with the lid on the jar but not sealed tight. After a day, you should see small bubbles; if you don't, let it sit out for another day, then refrigerate it.

10 You can eat this right away or wait about 2 weeks, for a little more funk to kick in. This will last almost indefinitely, though the flavor will intensify over time.

HOW-TO

1   Remove shaggy, bruised, or dirty outer leaves

2   Make a 2-inch (5 cm) slit in the cabbage core.

3   Use your hands to tear the cabbage in half. This is how it's traditionally done, because the leaves stay intact and you don't get little pieces of cabbage.

4   Make another 2-inch (5 cm) slit in the cabbage core and tear each half into quarters.

CONTINUES

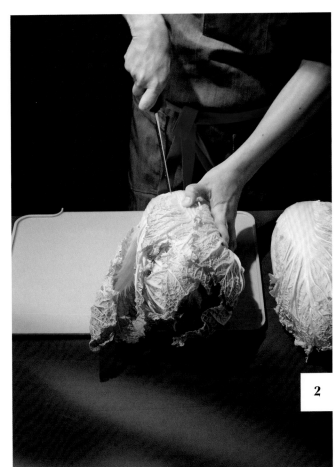

5 In your largest mixing bowl or stockpot, make the salt brine, making sure the salt is dissolved.

6 Swish the cabbage quarters in the brine, making sure all the leaves are coated with salt water.

7 Shake off the salt water and then toss the salt generously and with force in between all the cabbage leaves, aiming to get every surface lightly covered, even down where the leaf meets the core. Let the salted quarters sit for about 6 hours, either in a bowl under pressure or in large zip-top bags, then rinse them.

8 While the cabbage sits, prep the remaining ingredients.

9 To make the slurry, whisk the water and sticky rice flour continuously over medium heat until it begins to thicken and bubble and pull away from the sides. It should look like thick paste.

10 Once the slurry has cooled completely, use your largest mixing bowl or a stockpot to combine the ingredients for the marinade.

CONTINUES

11   As you make the marinade,
drain off any liquid that may have
accumulated from the vegetables,
especially the peppers and onions.

12   Mix everything together with
your hands. Plastic gloves are a wise
investment for this step, or you'll have
stained, tender hands from all the
chiles.

13   Put a cabbage quarter directly on
top of the marinade, then use your
hands to smear and slather a thin
layer of the marinade between all the
leaves, making sure to get into the
crevices near the core and the outside
layer.

14   Fold the cabbage quarter over on
itself into a little package. Pack the
quarters into mason jars, or better
still, an old gallon pickle jar.

BAECHU GUTJEORI

QUICK CHOPPED-CABBAGE KIMCHI

This has become my favorite kimchi to keep in my refrigerator. Not only does it taste great, but it's already cut and ready to plate for the table at any time! *Gutjeori* means something like "tossed," because we're making a quick, less seasoned, less fermented version of Baechu Kimchi (page 102) with already chopped cabbage. (Traditionally you'd use the outer napa cabbage leaves you toss away while making the baechu kimchi to make this.) Because of the high demand for kimchi at Insa, we usually make about eighty heads of this kimchi a week. The flavor is not as deep as Baechu Kimchi, but this is just as good in its own way: lighter, more like a salad, and best eaten fresh, within a week. You can cut this recipe in half, or make it with bok choy, green cabbage, or hearty lettuces like romaine—but just don't salt the greens first, and be sure to eat lettuce gutjeori within a day or two.

Korean supermarkets like H Mart usually sell brightly colored "kimchi boxes," which have plastic inserts that slide down to keep air from the kimchi. They also stack neatly in the fridge. You don't *need* one, but if you make a lot of kimchi, they're handy (and fun).

Makes 1 gallon (3.8 L)

- 2 large (3 pounds/1.4 kg each) napa cabbages
- 1 cup (240 g) kosher salt
- 1½ cups (180 g) gochugaru
- ¼ cup (25 g) minced peeled fresh ginger
- ¼ cup (35 g) minced garlic
- 3 tablespoons salted shrimp (optional, but recommended)
- 1 tablespoon fish sauce
- 2 bunches scallions, cut into 2-inch (5 cm) pieces

1. Tear each cabbage into long quarters (see instructions for Baechu Kimchi, page 104) and slice horizontally every 2 inches (5 cm). Cut the thicker part, toward the bottom, a bit smaller.

2. In your largest mixing bowl, mix and rub salt gently into the cabbage until it's nicely coated. Let the cabbage sit, covered, for 3 hours.

3. Rinse the cabbage well under running water and drain thoroughly.

4. Place the rest of the ingredients in a mixing bowl with the drained, chopped cabbage and mix everything together with gloved hands until the cabbage is well coated.

5. Add more salt or other seasoning to your liking.

6. Put the kimchi in a large nonreactive container and press it down to remove the air between the leaves. Let it sit, covered, at room temperature overnight, then refrigerate.

7. You can eat this immediately or after a few days, though this kimchi is best eaten within a week.

SEE HOW-TO ON FOLLOWING PAGES

HOW-TO

1 Quarter the cabbages lengthwise following the instructions on page 104.

2 Cut the quarters into 2-inch (5 cm) strips, and the thicker parts near the core slightly smaller.

3 Pile the sliced cabbage in your largest mixing bowl and sprinkle on the salt.

4 Toss and mix the cabbage with your hands until all the pieces are covered with salt. Let it sit, covered, for 3 hours, then rinse it and drain it well, shaking off excess water.

5 Add the gochugaru, ginger, garlic, salted shrimp, fish sauce, and scallions.

6 Mix everything well with your hands. (If you have gloves, wear them to protect your hands from the chiles.)

7 Store refrigerated in a nonreactive container.

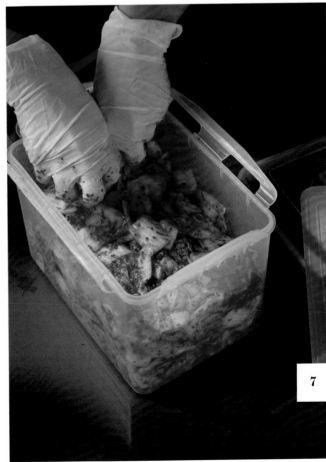

NABAK KIMCHI

SLICED RADISH AND CABBAGE WATER KIMCHI

This is named after the Korean term for slicing vegetables into non-uniform pieces, *nabak nabak*. It is also a great way to use up radishes and cabbage lingering in your crisper. Like Dongchimi (page 119), this is a water-based kimchi, and everything I said about Dongchimi applies: The radishes and cabbage are super cooling in summer, but the cold kimchi brine is almost as refreshing. In summer, I use it to make cold noodle dishes, and I take a swig of the brine in the morning for good health to begin the day!

Makes 1 gallon (3.8 L)

2 ½ pounds (1.2 kg) moo radish, scrubbed and peeled

1 ½ pounds (680 g/ about ½ large) napa cabbage, cored

¼ cup (60 g) kosher salt

3 tablespoons coarse sea salt

1 bunch scallions, white parts only, cut into 2-inch (5 cm) pieces

1 Holland chile, halved lengthwise

8 cloves garlic, minced

2-inch (5 cm) piece peeled fresh ginger, julienned

2 tablespoons gochugaru

1 tablespoon granulated sugar

1   Cut the radishes in half lengthwise. Then cut each half into thirds, lengthwise, then cut the thirds into ¼-inch (6 mm) slices. Set aside in a large mixing bowl.

2   Cut the cabbage in half lengthwise, then into 2-inch (5 cm) slices, and add them to the bowl with the radishes.

3   Toss 2 tablespoons of the kosher salt and the sea salt together with the vegetables and let them sit, loosely covered, for 3 hours at room temperature. Discard any water that accumulates in the bottom of the bowl and transfer the vegetables to a clean, large bowl, plastic storage container, or glass gallon jar with the scallions, chile, garlic, and ginger and set it aside.

4   Put the gochugaru in a cheesecloth bundle or tea ball, and add it to a large mixing bowl, stockpot, or glass gallon jar with 12 cups (3 L) water. After the gochugaru just begins to color the water red, about 5 minutes, remove the gochugaru, squeezing out the liquid (if it is in the cheesecloth) into the pot.

5   Dissolve the sugar and remaining 2 tablespoons kosher salt in the water, then pour the water mixture over the vegetables.

6   Stir it together and let it sit, loosely covered, at room temperature for 1 hour. Taste for seasoning, and add more salt and sugar as desired.

7   Let the vegetables sit, loosely covered, at room temperature for 24 hours, then move it to the refrigerator. It will keep for 2 months.

BUTCHU KIMCHI

GARLIC CHIVE KIMCH

With their flat, ribbon-like leaves, garlic chives make beautiful kimchi. Their funky, garlicky, oniony flavor is similar to ramps, which you could also use when they're in season. You can use this kimchi to spike many of your other favorite Korean dishes, like Kimchi Jeon (page 46) or Soondubu (page 202).

Makes 8 cups (2 L)

2 bunches
   garlic chives

2 tablespoons
   kosher salt

2 Holland chiles,
   seeded and
   thinly sliced

2 Korean green
   chiles, seeded and
   thinly sliced

1 cup (120 g)
   gochugaru

⅓ cup (75 ml)
   fish sauce

2 tablespoons
   minced garlic

1   Trim the root ends of the garlic chives, but keep them whole. Gently wash the garlic chives under running water, then rinse and drain them.

2   In a mixing bowl, toss the chives with the salt and let them sit for 1 hour, then drain off any liquid and rinse the chives under running water.

3   Combine the remaining ingredients in a mixing bowl with the rinsed chives and ½ cup (120 ml) water, making sure the chives are coated with the marinade.

4   Let the chives sit, covered, in the refrigerator for 2 days before serving. They will keep in the refrigerator for 3 to 4 weeks.

DONGCHIMI

WHOLE RADISH WATER KIMCHI

This refreshing, old-fashioned kimchi is white, as in made without red chiles, and water-based, made by fermenting salted moo radish covered in water for several weeks before you eat it. I like to say it keeps on giving: You get the funk and cooling crunch of the radishes, and the water itself becomes the refreshing, seasoned chilled broth for the chilled noodles on page 242 or any other dish you want to embellish. This is a must-make dish if you're into kimchi! Serve it on warm nights, when it tastes even more refreshing, cooling, and delicious.

NOTE: For this dish, young (as in smaller) and very fresh (as in not soft or wilting) radish is ideal.

Kimchi is often assumed to be hot and spicy and red with chiles, but it doesn't have to be. Koreans have been making kimchi since the time of the Three Kingdoms in China in the third century, several hundred years before chile peppers arrived in Korea. There are many white kimchis, like this one and Nabak (page 114). When I taste it, I can almost taste the origins of kimchi, just water and salt and time.

Makes 1 gallon (3.8 L)

3 pounds (1.4 kg) moo radish (see Note)

⅓ cup (40 g) kosher salt

2 scallions, blanched in boiling water

1 Asian pear, peeled, cored, and cut into quarters

5 cloves garlic, crushed

1-inch (2.5 cm) piece peeled fresh ginger, cut into three pieces

1 Korean green chile, halved lengthwise, seeds and membrane removed

1 Clean the radishes well by scrubbing them under running water. Let them dry completely.

2 Working in a mixing bowl, rub the salt all over the radishes.

3 Put the salted radish in a large nonreactive container and let sit, loosely covered, at room temperature for 4 to 5 days. (A large glass jar with a screw top is ideal.)

4 Add the remaining ingredients to the jar and cover with 12 cups (2.8 L) cold water.

5 Give the mixture a stir and taste the broth: It should taste like seasoned water, so add more salt if needed.

6 Let the jar sit at room temperature, loosely covered, for 24 hours, then keep it in the refrigerator for at least 2 and preferably 3 weeks before serving.

7 To serve the dongchimi, remove the radishes from the liquid and cut them into slices, or use the liquid in soups and stews. It will keep in the refrigerator for 3 months.

KKAKDUGI

CUBED MOO RADISH KIMCHI

This is a very easy and popular Korean radish kimchi, loved for its crunch and balanced flavor. Moo radish, the pale green, slightly spicy Korean radish shown on page 10, is similar to daikon, which makes a fine substitute, though moo cubes are sweeter and denser and go great with pork. This is best eaten before it gets strongly fermented and mushy, when the odor is strong and so is the taste. When it is funky, however, it is still great for cooking, and you can add it to Kimchi Jjigae (page 206) or the Korean version of bone broth (page 226).

Some people like to add glutinous rice flour slurry to this dish, like in Baechu Kimchi on page 102, as it is said to provide extra body to the end result. To add it, follow the instructions for Baechu Kimchi but use half the flour and water.

Makes 3 quarts (2.8 L)

5 pounds (2.3 kg) moo radish, peeled and cut into ½-inch (12 mm) cubes

3 tablespoons kosher salt

2 tablespoons granulated sugar

2 tablespoons plus ½ cup (60 g) gochugaru

3 tablespoons minced garlic

2 tablespoons minced peeled fresh ginger

2 tablespoons salted shrimp

2 teaspoons fish sauce

3 scallions, thinly sliced (optional)

1   Toss the moo radish cubes with the salt in a nonreactive mixing bowl or container and set them aside for 2 hours—they will release a lot of liquid.

2   Drain off half of the liquid and stir in the remaining ingredients. (Taste and add up to another tablespoon of sugar, if desired.)

3   Let the radish cubes sit, covered, at room temperature for 24 hours (or 2 days, if it is really cold outside and the temperature in your kitchen is cool), then store them in glass or nonreactive containers in the refrigerator.

4   These can be eaten right away, and are best consumed within 4 to 5 weeks.

SEE HOW-TO ON FOLLOWING PAGES

HOW-TO

1 Trim off the ends of the radish.

2 Peel it. (If your radish is in great shape, just scrub it—no need to peel.)

3 Cut the radish into ½-inch (12 mm) slices.

4 Cut the slices crosswise to make ½-inch (12 mm) cubes.

5 Put the cubes in a mixing bowl and toss them with the salt, sugar, and 2 tablespoons of gochugaru.

6 Let the mixture sit for 2 hours at room temperature while preparing the rest of the ingredients.

CONTINUES

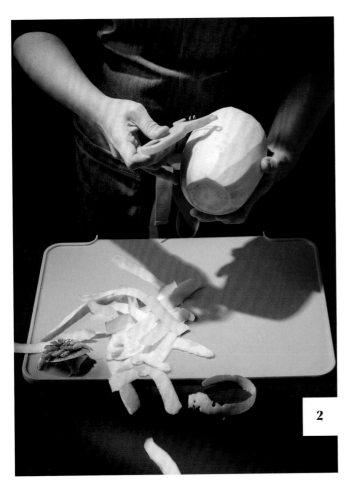

7 Drain off half of the liquid that has accumulated at the bottom of the bowl.

8 Fold in the remaining ingredients.

9 Toss the ingredients with your hands, and taste a cube for seasoning. If it is very bitter, mix in a tablespoon more sugar.

10 Pack the radish cubes and any liquid into a container and let it sit at room temperature for 24 hours, then refrigerate.

OI-SO-BEGI

STUFFED CUCUMBER KIMCHI

This stuffed cucumber kimchi is fun to serve and especially delicious in the summer. I like to chop it up and add it to cold noodle dishes as a crunchy condiment. This is a quick kimchi—don't try to let it ferment for a long time, or it will spoil and turn into mush.

Makes about 10 stuffed cucumbers

2 pounds (910 g/
   about 10) Kirby
   or Persian
   cucumbers

½ cup (120 g)
   kosher salt

1 cup (100 g)
   garlic chives,
   cut into ½-inch
   (12 mm) pieces

4 cloves garlic,
   minced

1 small carrot,
   julienned

½ cup (60 g)
   gochugaru

2 tablespoons
   fish sauce

1 tablespoon
   granulated sugar

1   Remove the tips from the cucumbers and pat the exposed ends dry. Put them in large zip-top bag with the salt, tossing to make sure the cucumbers are covered, and refrigerate the bag overnight.

2   The next day, rinse the cucumbers well and pat them dry.

3   Cut the cucumbers lengthwise in an X-shape, but do not cut all the way through the cucumber: leave a 1-inch (2.5 cm) edge at one end of the cucumber intact so that they still hold together.

4   In a mixing bowl, combine the rest of the ingredients with ¼ cup (60 ml) water to make the stuffing.

5   Use your hands to stuff each of the cucumbers with the stuffing. Layer the stuffed cucumbers in large glass jar or nonreactive container and refrigerate overnight.

6   Keep refrigerated and eat within 1 week.

KKETNIP KIMCHI

PERILLA KIMCHI

This kimchi makes for a delicious *banchan* and a very special treat to grace your Korean table. Picking up one delicate piece of pickled perilla leaf and wrapping it around some hot rice using only a pair of chopsticks is a skill innate to all Koreans. (For everyone else, practice makes perfect.) Perilla leaves, also known as sesame leaves, are the Korean version of shiso, with smoother edges and larger leaves. They're both in the mint family, and in the same way that there are different kinds of basil, there are different types of perilla or shiso, which are found in shades of green to purple and in various sizes. It's easy to grow your own, and you can collect seeds each fall for the next year.

Serves 8 to 10

2 ounces (55 g) perilla or shiso leaves (about 50 leaves)

3 tablespoons fish sauce

2 tablespoons honey

¼ cup (60 ml) soy sauce

⅓ cup (40 g) gochugaru

1 medium white onion, thinly sliced

3 tablespoons minced garlic

2 tablespoons minced peeled fresh ginger

1 small carrot, grated or julienned

1 Holland chile, halved lengthwise, seeds removed, and thinly sliced

1 tablespoon toasted sesame seeds

1   Wash the perilla leaves thoroughly and let them dry completely.

2   In a medium bowl, combine the remaining ingredients to make the seasoning paste.

3   Make a stack of 2 to 3 perilla leaves, then spread 1 to 2 teaspoons of the seasoning on top of the stack. Place the stacks on top of each other in a glass or plastic airtight container and store them in the fridge. The leaves will keep for several weeks in the refrigerator.

OJINGEOJEOT

SALTED PRESERVED SQUID IN SPICY SAUCE

Talk about an intense fermentation flavor! Perhaps this is not technically a kimchi, which generally applies to vegetables, but I use this spicy preserved squid the same way—served as *banchan* or a condiment to provide balance or brighten a dish. You can even use some of this preserved squid to make the Baechu Kimchi on page 102 instead of the salted shrimp.

Makes 12 ounces (340 g)

1 pound (455 g)
  fresh squid,
  cleaned (see
  Note, page 150)

¼ cup (60 g)
  kosher salt

⅔ cup (165 ml)
  gochugaru

⅓ cup (75 ml) brown
  rice syrup

1 tablespoon
  fish sauce

10 cloves garlic,
  thinly sliced

2 Holland chiles,
  thinly sliced

2 Korean long
  green chiles,
  thinly sliced

Toasted sesame
  seeds

Sesame oil, for
  drizzling

1   Rinse the squid under cold running water and pat dry. Separate the tentacles from the bodies, and if the tentacles are really large, cut them in half (you want to be able to pick them up with chopsticks and eat them).

2   Place the squid in a nonreactive baking dish and rub the salt into the bodies and the tentacles. Let sit, at room temperature, for 1 hour, then refrigerate overnight.

3   The next day, rinse all the salt off the squid and let it drain well in a colander set over a bowl or the sink. Pat the squid dry and cut the bodies into thin strips.

4   In a small mixing bowl, combine the gochugaru, brown rice syrup, fish sauce, garlic, chiles, and sesame seeds. Taste for seasoning and add more salt, fish sauce, or brown rice syrup as needed.

5   Add the squid to the bowl and mix well, ensuring the pieces are fully coated, then pack them into a glass jar and store in the refrigerator.

6   You can eat this right away, drizzled with some sesame oil, though the flavors will continue to develop over time. It lasts in the refrigerator for about 3 weeks.

Many consider BBQ *the* quintessential Korean food, though a meal based around grilled meat has only become a common thing in my lifetime. Now, along with *chimek* (fried chicken and beer), it's one of the most popular styles of eating out in the country. Koreans don't say they are going to a Korean BBQ, per se—they usually say they are going to a *gogi jip*—a meat house!

This is not American BBQ, which is slow and low: This is thin and quick. A live coal fire (*sut bul*) is not necessary, but it is preferred by most. To that end, feel free to cook K-BBQ any way you can: on a park grill, on a tabletop electric grill from a Korean market, on a pan on the stove (with windows open and a fan on—there's a lot of smoke!), or even in the broiler. In fact, before most Koreans owned ovens, we had little broilers, which we used for fish or meat. Koreans traditionally like their meat cooked through, but the really important thing is to get some char, a little caramelization, which you can achieve on any cooking surface.

A couple of important things to think about if you're hosting a Korean BBQ dinner party: BBQ is the main player, but it's not just about the meat. You need at least three *banchan*, including one kimchi, being mindful of color and texture. You need a big basket of fresh, beautiful lettuces and herbs, and a few of the condiments on page 157. You also have bowls of rice on the table—traditionally everyone had one, but now you can do just a few—and maybe a shared *jjigae* (stew) or a bowl of noodles, the customary way to end a meal of BBQ. To eat the BBQ by way of a *ssam* (wrap), you smear a little ssam jang (see page 157) on the lettuce, then lay in meat and rice and wrap tightly. It's actually a healthy way to eat a meal.

KOREAN BARBEQUE

YANGNYUM KALBI
MARINATED SHORT RIBS

The epitome of Korean barbecue is *kalbi*—fatty and beefy short ribs sliced very thin, marinated for 48 hours in soy sauce, sugar, and a little grated Asian pear, then charred on the grill. There's something so satisfying about eating meat that tender and that sweet—in fact, my kids call it "meat candy." Buy the short ribs pre-sliced from a Korean supermarket, if possible, then marinate them yourself, to make the dish even easier. (This is what I do at home.) If not, see pages 136–139 for directions on cutting the meat yourself. It's a fair amount of work, yes, but it is definitely impressive. When you grill these, grill them to your liking—medium-rare or totally cooked through. Mainly you want to make sure the meat gets at least a little char, so that the sweet sauce caramelizes on the beef.

Serves 4 to 6

FOR THE
SHORT RIBS

1 cup (240 ml)
soy sauce

2 tablespoons
kosher salt

1 Asian pear,
peeled, cored,
and grated
or pureed

1 cup (240 g)
granulated sugar

1 medium white
onion, grated

½ cup (95 g)
grated peeled
fresh ginger

½ cup (70 g)
minced garlic

2 tablespoons
canola oil,
plus extra
for greasing

2 pounds (910 g)
boneless short
ribs sliced
¼ inch (6 mm)
thick (see pages
136-139)

FOR SERVING

Lettuces and Herbs
(page 157)

Ssam Jang
(page 157)

Scallion Salad
(page 157)

2 to 3 Banchan
(see pages
16-131)

Rice (page 15)

1 In a large zip-top bag or nonreactive storage container, mix together the soy sauce, salt, pear, sugar, onion, ginger, garlic, oil, and 1½ cups (360 ml) water until well blended.

2 Add the short ribs, turning them so they are well covered, and let them marinate for 2 days, or at least overnight. (Do not let them marinate for more than 48 hours, as the meat will begin to break down.)

3 Heat a skillet or grill pan over high heat. Coat the bottom with a little oil, just enough so the meat won't stick, then add the meat in a single layer without crowding the pan; you don't want the meat to steam. (You may need to do this in batches.)

4 Cook the meat until it is charred on one side, about 2 to 3 minutes. Then flip and cook to your desired degree of doneness—less than a minute more for rare, a few minutes more for medium or well-done.

5 Cut the meat into bite-size pieces and serve immediately with the lettuces and herbs, ssam jang, scallion salad, banchan, and rice.

SEE HOW-TO ON FOLLOWING PAGES

HOW-TO

1 Buy bone-in beef short ribs. You'll need to start with about 5 pounds (2.3 kg) of meat, usually two pieces, because much of the weight is bone.

2 Each piece of meat has about 3 wide flat bones. Turn each piece on its side and cut along the bones. You'll end up with 6 pieces. (If you have boneless, just cut it into 3 even pieces.)

3 Trim off most of the fat cap from each rectangle.

4 Remove the silverskin by angling the knife up under the silverskin and working it off. When you braise short ribs the silverskin melts away, but when you quickly grill them it gets tough and will warp the slices of meat if not removed.

CONTINUES

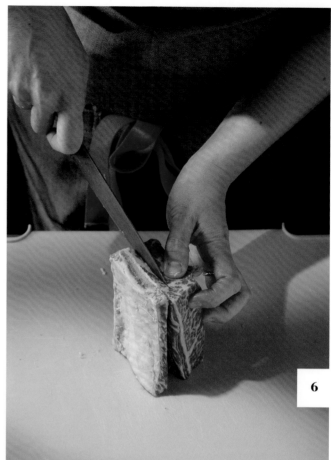

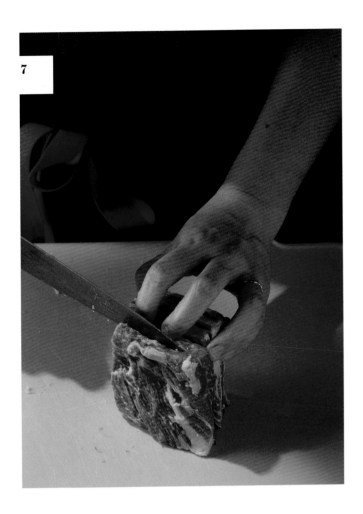

7

5 Separate the bone slightly from the meat: Run your knife along the bone in between the bone and the meat, making sure not to cut all the way through—leave about ¼ inch (6 cm) of space toward the end so the bone is still slightly attached to the meat. (If you have boneless, skip to the next step.)

6 Turn the pieces so that the area where the bone is still attached to the meat is facing up. Cut a slit downward a third of the way from the side with the bone, again making sure not to cut all the way through the meat.

7 Flip the rectangle of meat over and make another slit about two-thirds of the way in from the side with the bone, again making sure not to cut all the way through the meat.

8 The goal is to cut the meat with 3 slits like an accordion, so that you can open it up into one long, flat piece. It's the same principle as butterflying a piece of meat, just with a few more cuts.

9 Score the meat with a crosshatch pattern. This helps the marinade penetrate the meat, which will tenderize it and allow it to cook more quickly.

LA-STYLE KALBI
FLANKEN-CUT MARINATED SHORT RIBS

When large numbers of Koreans first moved to Los Angeles in the 1970s, the only short ribs they could find were cut in the German-Jewish style, for the dish called *flanken*. For traditional *kalbi* we use what's called "English cut": The ribs are cut into thick pieces with the bone, with one bone per piece. For flanken-style ribs, the ribs are cut across the rib bones into ½-inch (12 mm) slices, and each slice is dotted with three or four short sections of bone. Over the years, LA-style kalbi became its own thing, known in New York and even Korea. Even my father, who came to the United States as an adult, would make it in New York when I was growing up. The marinade here is very similar to the ones for Bulgogi (page 185) and regular kalbi (page 134), and in fact you can use either of those if you have them on hand.

NOTE: Ask your butcher for flanken or flanken-cut short ribs, or if you're in a Korean supermarket, look for the words "LA Kalbi."

Serves 4 to 6

FOR THE KALBI

1 medium white onion, roughly chopped

1 medium Asian pear, peeled, cored, and roughly chopped

2 tablespoons minced garlic

2 teaspoons minced peeled fresh ginger

¾ cup (180 ml) soy sauce

½ cup (100 g) granulated sugar

2 tablespoons mirin

1 teaspoon freshly ground black pepper

2 tablespoons sesame oil

2½ pounds (1.2 kg) flanken-style short ribs (see Note)

Canola oil, for greasing

FOR SERVING

Lettuces and Herbs (page 157)

Ssam Jang (page 157)

Scallion Salad (page 157)

2 to 3 Banchan (see pages 16-131)

Rice (page 15)

1 Put the onion and pear in a food processor or blender and process until both are pureed. Transfer the puree to a large mixing bowl.

2 Add the garlic, ginger, soy sauce, sugar, mirin, black pepper, sesame oil, and ½ cup (120 ml) water to the bowl and stir until well combined. Taste for seasoning, adding more of any ingredient as desired. Transfer to a large zip-top bag or nonreactive storage container and set aside.

3 Rinse off the short ribs in cold water, making sure there are no little bits of bones left on the meat. Pat them dry and add them to the marinade, making sure all the meat is covered in the mixture. Let them marinate overnight in the refrigerator.

4 Heat a skillet or grill pan over high heat. Coat the bottom with a little oil, just enough so the steak won't stick, then add the meat in a single layer without crowding the pan; you don't want the meat to steam. (You may need to do this in batches.)

5 Cook the meat until it is charred on one side, about 2 to 3 minutes. Then flip and cook to your desired degree of doneness—less than a minute more for rare, a few minutes more for medium or well-done.

6 Cut the meat into bite-size pieces and serve immediately with the lettuces and herbs, ssam jang, scallion salad, banchan, and rice.

SAMGYUPSAL

SLICED PORK BELLY

If you can, visit a fancy butcher shop to get an heirloom breed of pork with lots of flavor for this BBQ—it's cooked plain, so good-quality pork makes all the difference. Note that pork belly is in such high demand these days, you might need to order it in advance. I prefer to render out a lot of the fat and cook this till it's almost well-done—with a little bit of char and crisp—though some people prefer it soft and fatty.

You can K-BBQ any meat, not just the cuts I've listed here, including beef brisket, tongue, sirloin steak, flap steak, pork collar, and so on and so forth.

Serves 2 to 4

FOR THE PORK BELLY	FOR SERVING
1 pound (455 g) boneless, skinless pork belly	Lettuces and Herbs (page 157)
Canola oil, for greasing	Scallion Salad (page 157)
	Ssam Jang (page 157)
	Soybean Powder (page 157)
	Sesame Oil and Salt (page 157)
	2 to 3 Banchan (see pages 16–131)
	Rice (page 15)

1   Trim off any excess fat from the pork belly and slice the pork belly into ½-inch (12 mm) slices, like thick-cut bacon. Score it crosswise with a sharp knife into ½-inch (12 mm) cross hatches.

2   Heat a skillet or grill pan over high heat. Coat the bottom with a little oil, just enough so the pork won't stick, then add the meat in a single layer without crowding the pan; you don't want the meat to steam. (You may need to do this in batches.)

3   Cook the meat until it is charred on one side, about 2 to 3 minutes. Then flip and cook to your desired degree of doneness—about 2 to 3 minutes more for medium or well-done.

4   Cut the meat into bite-size pieces, and serve immediately with the lettuces and herbs, scallion salad, ssam jang, soybean powder, sesame oil and salt, banchan, and rice.

DWEJI BULGOGI

SPICY MARINATED PORK BUTT

This is thinly sliced marinated pork that's stir-fried, just like beef bulgogi (page 185)—but this version is spicy. You can also make this with pork belly, shoulder, loin, collar, or just about any cut of pork you have on hand. You could scale this dish up and serve it as a main dish, as you would with beef bulgogi.

NOTE: It's much easier to thinly slice meat by hand if you partially freeze it so that it is firm but still sliceable—about an hour or so.

Serves 2 to 4

FOR THE PORK

1 small Spanish onion, thinly sliced

2 tablespoons gochugaru

3 tablespoons gochujang

2 tablespoons minced garlic

1 tablespoon minced peeled fresh ginger

2 tablespoons mirin

2 tablespoons rice wine vinegar

¼ teaspoon freshly ground black pepper

2 tablespoons packed brown sugar

1 tablespoon soy sauce

1 tablespoon sesame oil

1 pound (455 g) boneless pork butt

Canola oil, for greasing

FOR SERVING

Lettuces and Herbs (page 157)

Scallion Salad (page 157)

Ssam Jang (page 157)

Soybean Powder (page 157)

2 to 3 Banchan (see pages 16-131)

Rice (page 15)

1 In a zip-top bag or nonreactive storage container, mix together the onion, gochugaru, gochujang, garlic, ginger, mirin, rice wine vinegar, black pepper, brown sugar, soy sauce, and sesame oil.

2 Slice the pork butt as thinly as you can (see Note). Add the sliced pork to the marinade, mixing to ensure it is well covered, and let sit, at room temperature, for at least 30 minutes or refrigerate it overnight.

3 Heat a skillet or grill pan over high heat. Coat the bottom with a little oil, just enough so the pork won't stick, then add the meat in a single layer without crowding the pan; you don't want the meat to steam. (You may need to do this in batches.)

4 Cook the meat until it is charred on one side, about 2 to 3 minutes. Then flip and cook it to your desired degree of doneness—about 2 to 3 minutes more for medium or well-done.

5 Cut the meat into bite-size pieces and serve immediately with the lettuces and herbs, scallion salad, ssam jang, soybean powder, banchan, and rice.

BOL SAL

CURED PORK JOWL

Pork jowl is a traditional cut that many Koreans love to grill—it's just beautiful fatty pork jowl, lightly cured in a little salt. You'll most likely have to order the pork jowl from a butcher if you can't get to a Korean market such as H Mart. This can be scaled up as you like.

Most of these K-BBQ recipes call for 1 pound (455 g) of meat, which feeds two. Multiply the quantity as you need, or, better still for a party, prepare a few different kinds of meat.

Serves 2 to 4

FOR THE PORK

1 teaspoon kosher salt

1 pork jowl (about 1 pound/455 g), trimmed of extra fat

Canola oil, for greasing

FOR SERVING

Lettuces and Herbs (page 157)

Scallion Salad (page 157)

Ssam Jang (page 157)

Soybean Powder (page 157)

Sesame Oil and Salt (page 157)

2 to 3 Banchan (see pages 16–131)

Rice (page 15)

1   Sprinkle the salt on both sides of the pork jowl and let it sit, uncovered, in the refrigerator overnight.

2   Slice the jowl into ¼-inch (6 mm) slices.

3   Heat a skillet or grill pan over high heat. Coat the bottom with a little oil, just enough so the pork won't stick, then add the meat in a single layer without crowding the pan; you don't want the meat to steam. (You may need to do this in batches.)

4   Cook the meat until it is charred on one side, about 2 to 3 minutes. Then flip and cook to your desired degree of doneness—about 2 to 3 minutes more for medium or well-done.

5   Cut the meat into bite-size pieces and serve immediately with the lettuces and herbs, scallion salad, ssam jang, soybean powder, sesame oil and salt, banchan, and rice.

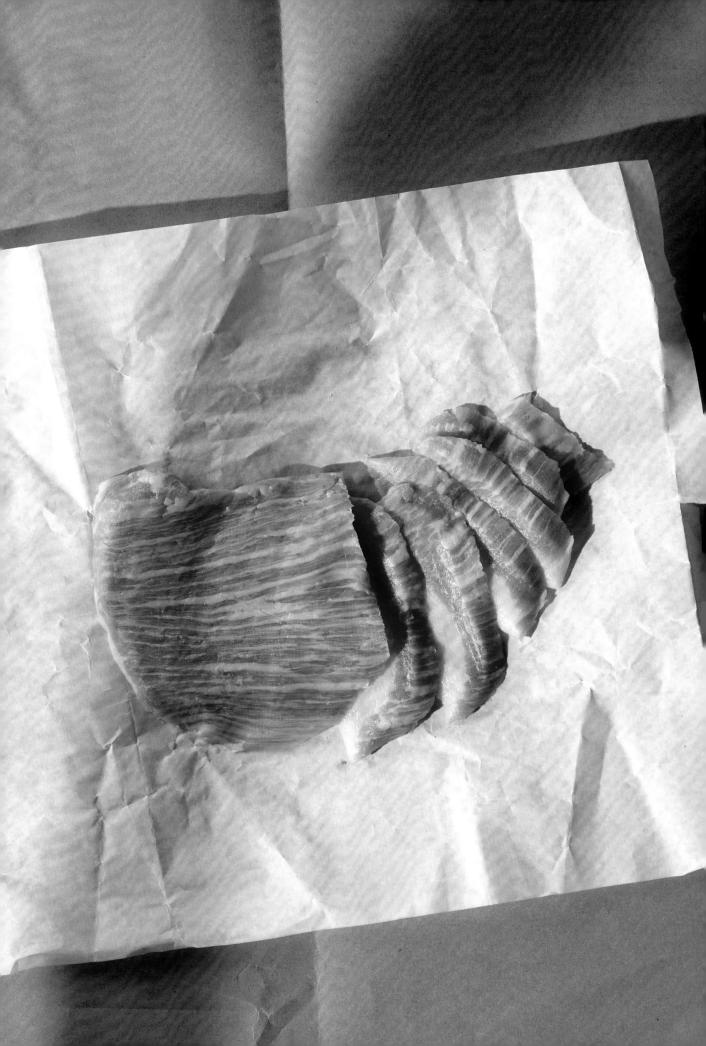

DWEJi KALBi

GOCHUJANG-GLAZED BABY BACK RIBS

Though baby backs aren't a tradition in Korea, these spicy-sweet glazed ribs definitely have the flavor of the old country. My father used to make spare ribs in a similar fashion on city park grills on Sundays, his one day off. If we were pressed for time, he would just cook the ribs for an hour in the oven so that they were cooked through, then brush on the glaze to finish them on the grill, which is how I make them now.

Serves 2 to 4

1 rack (about
  3½ pounds/1.6 kg)
  baby back ribs

1 tablespoon
  kosher salt

2 teaspoons
  granulated sugar

¼ cup (60 ml)
  gochujang

¼ to ⅓ cup
  (60 to 75 ml) rice
  wine vinegar

3 tablespoons
  gochugaru

3 tablespoons
  minced garlic

2 tablespoons
  minced peeled
  fresh ginger

2 tablespoons
  soy sauce

2 tablespoons honey

1 teaspoon freshly
  ground black
  pepper

1   Preheat the oven to 400°F (205°C).

2   Cut the rack of ribs in half in between the middle ribs. In a small mixing bowl, combine the salt and sugar. Season the ribs evenly all over with the salt-sugar blend and set them aside.

3   Tightly double-wrap each rack half in heavy-duty aluminum foil and place the packets on a baking sheet.

4   Cook the rib packets for 1 hour. Turn the packets over a few times with tongs during the process so that the ribs cook evenly, making sure not to pierce the foil.

5   While the ribs cook, make the glaze. In a small mixing bowl, whisk together the gochujang, ¼ cup (60 ml) vinegar, the gochugaru, garlic, ginger, soy sauce, honey, and black pepper until smooth. Add more vinegar as necessary until it has the consistency of barbecue sauce. Set aside.

6   Remove the packets from the oven and let them rest for at least 10 minutes. Turn the oven to broil or prepare a grill for a medium-hot fire.

7   Carefully open the foil packets, remove the ribs, and discard the foil and any collected juices. Place the racks on the baking sheet and baste them with the glaze. Broil them, turning and basting them with the sauce once or twice, until they are sizzling and lightly charred, about 4 to 5 minutes. To finish these on a grill, place the ribs directly over the fire and cook until they are sizzling and lightly charred, turning and basting them with the sauce from time to time but keeping the lid closed as much as possible between bastings.

8   Remove the ribs to a cutting board and let them rest for about 5 minutes. Cut them into individual ribs and serve immediately with any remaining sauce on the side.

SAEWOO AND OJiNGO

SHRIMP AND SQUID

This treatment is best for fresh shrimp or squid that have not already been frozen, if you can find them. Dip them into ssam jang or a bright, seafood-friendly sauce like my Kimchi Vinaigrette on page 157. If you are lucky enough to live within a few hours of a coastline, you should also look for locally caught versions.

NOTE: To clean your own squid, gently pull the tentacles and head from the tube-like body. Cut the tentacles off right below the eyes and discard the guts. (You don't have to remove the skin from the tubes, as it's edible, but if you want pale white rings, you can easily strip it off.) To cut the tubes into strips, slice the tubes lengthwise from top to bottom with a sharp knife. Rinse under running water and pat dry. If the tubes are thick—more than ¼ inch (6 mm) thick—gently score the inside of each one in a crosshatch pattern with a sharp knife.

Serves 4 to 6

FOR THE SHRIMP

2 tablespoons canola oil

1 pound (450 g) fresh medium-size shrimp, peeled and deveined OR 1 pound (455 g) fresh, unfrozen squid bodies and tentacles, cleaned (see Note)

Kosher salt

FOR SERVING

Lettuces and Herbs (page 157)

Scallion Salad (page 157)

Kimchi Vinaigrette (page 157)

Ssam Jang (page 157; optional)

2 to 3 Banchan (see pages 16-131)

Rice (page 15)

1   In a large skillet or grill pan, heat 1 tablespoon of the oil over medium heat.

2   Season the shrimp or squid lightly with salt on both sides. Toss with the remaining tablespoon of oil to coat.

3   When the skillet is hot, add the shrimp or squid. Cook until they just begin to curl, about a minute per side, then remove them to a serving platter. Cut the squid, if using, into bite-size pieces.

4   Serve immediately with the lettuces and herbs, scallion salad, kimchi vinaigrette or ssam jang, banchan, and rice.

NAKJI

OCTOPUS

I love octopus—so meaty and so sweet. In Korea they wouldn't serve this as part of BBQ, but they do eat it along the coast, boiled and dipped in a gochujang sauce, like the one on page 241. (You can do the same thing with shrimp and squid.) Nearly all octopus in the United States is frozen—defrost it first if you have the time, or just rinse the frozen octopus off and place it right in the boiling water, letting it cook a few seconds longer.

Serves 4 to 6

FOR THE OCTOPUS

1 small (12- to 16-ounce/340 to 455 g) whole octopus

2 tablespoons canola oil

Kosher salt

FOR SERVING

Lettuces and Herbs (page 157)

Kimchi Vinaigrette (page 157)

Scallion Salad (page 157)

Ssam Jang (page 157; optional)

2 to 3 Banchan (see pages 16-131)

Rice (page 15)

1   Preheat the oven to 250°F (120°C).

2   Bring a large saucepan of water to a boil over high heat. Add the octopus and let it cook for 1 minute, then remove it to a baking pan.

3   Place the octopus in the oven and let it cook until it is tender when you pierce it with the tip of a knife, about 2 to 3 hours.

4   Slice off the head and discard it, then separate each tentacle where it begins at the neck.

5   In a large skillet or grill pan, heat 1 tablespoon of the oil over medium heat.

6   Season the octopus tentacles liberally with salt on both sides. Toss with the remaining tablespoon of oil to coat.

7   When the skillet is hot, add the octopus. Cook until it is charred on both sides, about 3 minutes per side.

8   Cut the octopus tentacles into bite-size pieces, and serve immediately with the lettuces and herbs, kimchi vinaigrette or ssam jang, scallion salad, banchan, and rice.

PA MUCHIM

SCALLION SALAD

This salad can also be served as *banchan* with any meal, but its best use is on the BBQ table. I love to make *ssam* (a wrap) with any grilled meat, a little rice, and a big tangle of this salad. It really makes for a perfect bite! This can be easily multiplied for a crowd; just be careful with the salt.

Serves 2 to 4

1 bunch scallions

2 teaspoons rice wine vinegar

1 teaspoon gochugaru

1 teaspoon sesame oil

1 teaspoon sesame seeds

½ teaspoon kosher salt

½ teaspoon granulated sugar

1 Prepare a mixing bowl with clean water and a few cubes of ice. Set aside.

2 Trim the root ends and dry tops from the scallions. Cut the scallions into pieces about 2 inches (5 cm) long.

3 Slice each length of scallion vertically as thinly as you can to make thin strips. As you cut them, drop them into the ice water.

4 When all the scallions are cut, let them soak in the ice water for 20 to 30 minutes.

5 Drain the scallions well and pat them as dry as you can with paper towels. Set them aside while you make the dressing.

6 In a clean, dry mixing bowl, whisk together the vinegar, gochugaru, sesame oil, sesame seeds, salt, and sugar.

7 Add the scallions, tossing them until they are coated in the dressing. Serve immediately with BBQ or as banchan. This salad should be eaten the day it is made.

KIMCHI VINAIGRETTE

This is a dipping sauce for any kind of grilled seafood. We started to make it at the Good Fork long before I opened Insa, and it has since been perfected there by my friend Chef Rigo Vazquez. We always had a lot of kimchi juice left over, and instead of throwing it away, we'd use it in soups and sauces like using vinegar or any other acid. To that end, you can also use this dressing to make crudo or ceviche with thin slices of mahi-mahi or butterflied raw shrimp.

Makes about 2 cups (475 ml)

1 cup (240 ml) kimchi juice	1 scallion, white part only, chopped
2 tablespoons gochujang	¼ cup (40 g) chopped white onion or shallot
¼ cup (60 ml) rice wine vinegar	1 tablespoon minced peeled fresh ginger
2 tablespoons granulated sugar	½ cup (120 ml) canola oil
1 tablespoon kosher salt	

Combine all ingredients except the oil in a blender. With the blender on low, slowly drizzle in the oil until the vinaigrette emulsifies. Refrigerate for up to 5 days.

SANGCHU
LETTUCES AND HERBS

Think of this as making a floral arrangement with lettuces and herbs. Start with the very best and freshest leaf lettuces you can find in your backyard garden or farmers' market, and wash and dry them with care. (They are best when fluffy and bone dry, so give them ample time to dry before dinner.) The end result should be a bouquet of yellow, red, green, and light green. Traditionally you would have perilla leaf or shiso (see page 10), too, but feel free to use the herbs that you love and that are fresh: cilantro, basil, mint, anything goes.

KONG-GARU
SOYBEAN POWDER

This is traditionally served with any kind of BBQ pork. Look for roasted soybean powder in Asian supermarkets or online. There is also fermented soybean powder—you don't want that here. Serve it in two or more small bowls, with at least one on each side of the table.

CHAMGIREUM, SOGEUM
SESAME OIL AND SALT

This is traditionally served in small bowls at any kind of BBQ where the meat does not already have a marinade. You can stir the sesame oil and salt together to dissolve the salt slightly if you like, but I don't bother—instead I just dip a piece of meat into the bowl like a paint brush and drag it through the salt in the bowl.

SSAM JANG
SEASONED DOENGJANG SAUCE

This is my version of the ubiquitous, umami-packed Korean condiment. The name means wrapped (ssam) sauce (jang), and it's meant to be used anywhere delicious cooked things are wrapped in leafy greens and eaten out of hand. You can easily buy many brands of it in any Korean grocery, but it tastes much better made at home, and you can adjust it to your taste.

Makes about 1 cup (240 ml)

¾ cup (180 ml) doenjang	2 tablespoons honey
¼ cup (60 ml) gochujang	2 tablespoons sesame oil
2 cloves garlic, minced	1 tablespoon toasted sesame seeds
1 tablespoon grated peeled fresh ginger	

1   In a small mixing bowl, combine the doenjang, gochujang, garlic, ginger, honey, sesame oil, and sesame seeds until it becomes a smooth paste.

2   Taste for seasoning, and add more gochujang or honey as desired. This will last for at least 1 month in a tightly sealed container in the refrigerator.

In addition to ssam jang, other easy-to-prepare BBQ condiments include whole garlic cloves, sliced fresh chiles, plain gochuchang, and plain doenjang.

Years ago, the traditional meal for a normal Korean family like mine would have been *banchan*, rice, and soup. If you saw a mound of meat or a whole fish on the table, it meant something good had happened to your family, something to celebrate. While meat or seafood might have been added to a stew, it was rarely at the center of the table. And even when it was the center, it was still a healthful meal, with a table full of vegetable-based banchan side dishes.

Now that's all out the window. With the rise of the South Korean economy, and overall affluence around the country, a lot of the recipes in this chapter are everyday meals and anytime snacks for all Koreans, now found on menus of ordinary, everyday restaurants there and here in the United States. A dish built only around meat or fish is no longer special or rare, and with a few banchan it is still a balanced meal. In fact, if you're serving a traditional Korean meal for a party, a lot of the recipes in this chapter can be served as special banchan, too.

HAESANMUL & GOGI

SEAFOOD & MEAT

"HOT BAR"

SEAFOOD SAUSAGE

"Hot bar" is a snacky street food craze that hit Korea many years ago, as an extension of our longtime love of fish cakes like the ones in the *banchan* on page 60. They are formed into balls and shaped into rectangular corn dogs, which look like logs or bars—hence the name hot bar, I imagine—and often served on skewers. Sometimes people even stick in a thin piece of Spam (page 188) or other goodies before it's battered and fried. At Insa, where we call them Seafood Corn Dogs, we also serve them skewered on a chopstick and topped with a drizzle of ketchup and mayonnaise. If you want to dress them up, sprinkle them with slivered scallions and a mix of toasted white and black sesame seeds.

Serves 4 to 6 / Makes 4 dozen balls

1 pound (455 g) pollack

½ pound (225 g) shrimp

½ pound (225 g) squid

1 teaspoon minced garlic

4 teaspoons sake

2 teaspoons freshly ground black pepper

2 tablespoons kosher salt

1 tablespoon granulated sugar

½ cup (80 g) potato starch

½ cup (65 g) all-purpose flour

1 bunch scallions, 1 scallion sliced into thin slices on the bias and the remainder finely diced, white and green parts separated

1 small carrot, minced

2 tablespoons minced Korean green chile

2 tablespoons minced Holland chile

Vegetable oil, for frying

Ketchup and mayonnaise, for serving

1   Combine the pollack, shrimp, squid, garlic, sake, black pepper, salt, sugar, starch, flour, and the diced whites of the scallions in a blender or food processor and process until smooth.

2   Fold in the diced greens of the scallions, the carrot, and the chiles.

3   Fill a Dutch oven or heavy-bottomed pot about halfway with vegetable oil, then heat until it begins to shimmer and measures about 350°F (175°C). Line a baking sheet with paper towels.

4   Form the fish cake batter into hot dog shapes (or small round balls, about 1 tablespoon each) with oiled hands and then set them on a greased work surface or nonstick baking sheet.

5   Slip the fish cakes gently into the hot oil and cook them in batches, making sure not to crowd the pot, until they are golden brown and begin to float, about 2 to 3 minutes for balls or 3 or 4 minutes for logs. Remove them with a spider or slotted spoon to the paper towels.

6   Serve immediately with ketchup and mayonnaise.

GANJANG GAEJANG

SOY-MARINATED CRABS

This is a serious crab recipe, even for those who love crab. It's technically a pickled raw crab dish—most Koreans let it ferment at room temperature for a few days, but I prefer them quick-pickled and refrigerated. The main trick is not to make the pickling solution too salty, though a little salt is good. In fact, this dish, and the spicy crabs on page 164, are nicknamed "the rice thief" because they make you want to eat so much more rice. You should definitely serve these with individual bowls of rice for each diner.

NOTE: Before you clean the crabs, let them sit in the refrigerator for an hour or so to put them to sleep.

2 cups (480 ml) soy sauce

2-inch (5 cm) piece peeled fresh ginger, sliced

6 large cloves garlic, crushed

2 dried red chiles, such as Mexican chiles de árbol, crushed

1 fresh Holland chile, scored 2 to 3 times on each side

1 Granny Smith or Honeycrisp apple

3 tablespoons granulated sugar

6 live blue crabs (see Note)

1   Place all the ingredients except for the crabs in a medium saucepan. Add 4 cups (960 ml) water and bring just to a boil, then turn off the heat and let it cool completely.

2   Once the crabs are cleaned, pound the legs with a mallet (or clean wine bottle) to open the segments, which will allow the meat to soak up the marinade. Cut off the tips of the smaller legs, and place the crabs in a large mixing bowl.

3   Pour the cooled liquid over the cleaned crabs, and let them marinate in the refrigerator, covered, overnight.

4   The next day, remove the crabs from the liquid and set aside. Strain the marinade and discard any solids, then pour it into a medium saucepan with 2 cups (480 ml) water. Bring it to a boil, then turn off the heat and let the liquid cool, skimming any impurities.

5   Pour the cooled liquid over the crabs once again, then pack the crabs and the liquid into an airtight container and refrigerate.

6   Serve the crabs as soon as they are chilled or the very next day—the crabs won't keep longer than 3 days from the time you clean them.

YANGNYUM GAEJANG

SPICY MARINATED CRABS

For this spiced, marinated crab dish, I say skip cleaning fresh ones yourself and instead use flash-frozen, cleaned blue crabs that you find in the freezer aisle of Asian supermarkets. I especially like Tong Tong Bay's frozen seafood, as it's very good quality. Better still, the freezing process softens the shell so that eating them is easier, too. Just defrost them and let the crabs marinate for at least one hour at room temperature, then pop them in the refrigerator, where they will keep for up to three days, soaking up even more sauce as they do. Serve these with individual bowls of rice.

Serves 4

3 tablespoons
  soy sauce

¼ cup (30 g)
  gochugaru

1 tablespoon
  minced garlic

1 teaspoon minced
  peeled fresh ginger

1 tablespoon packed
  dark brown sugar

2 teaspoons toasted
  sesame seeds

1 teaspoon fish sauce

½ cup (50 g) thinly
  sliced scallions
  or leeks, white
  parts only

1 small carrot,
  julienned

1 pound (455 g)
  cleaned blue crabs
  (see Note, page 163)

1 Combine everything but the crabs in a small mixing bowl. Whisk until well combined and the sugar is dissolved.

2 Toss each crab with the sauce until it is coated, then place it in a large mixing bowl.

3 Once all the crabs are covered with the marinade, pour the remaining marinade over the crabs, and let the bowl sit out, covered, for 1 to 2 hours, then refrigerate it overnight.

4 Serve the crabs within 3 days.

KKANPOONG SAEWOO

CRISPY SWEET-AND-SOUR SHRIMP

This is what you order alongside Jjajang Myeon, on page 235, at Korean Chinese restaurants. It's your typical guilt-inducing, fried-and-bathed-in-sweet-sauce dish, but oh, it's so, so good. It is also easier to make at home than you might think: Just get the freshest, plumpest shrimp you can find and double-fry them, which makes them really crunchy and helps them stand up to the sauce. I like to serve this with a simple dipping sauce of rice wine vinegar and gochugaru.

Serves 4

Vegetable oil, for frying

½ cup (80 g) potato starch

1 large egg, beaten

1 pound (455 g) large shrimp, peeled and deveined

2 tablespoons soy sauce

2 tablespoons oyster sauce

1 tablespoon granulated sugar

2 tablespoons brown rice syrup

3 tablespoons rice wine vinegar

1 tablespoon fresh lemon juice

2 tablespoons mirin

2 tablespoons olive oil

4 to 5 dried hot red chiles, such as Mexican chiles de árbol

5 cloves garlic, thinly sliced

1-inch (2.5 cm) piece peeled fresh ginger, julienned

½ medium onion, finely diced

1 Holland chile, seeded and finely diced

1 Korean green chile, seeded and finely diced

1 scallion, thinly sliced, for garnish

1. Fill a Dutch oven or heavy-bottomed pot about halfway with vegetable oil, and heat it over medium-high heat until it begins to shimmer, to about 350°F (175°C). Line a baking sheet with paper towels.

2. While the oil heats, prepare two large mixing bowls, one with the potato starch and one with the egg. Toss the shrimp in the bowl with the potato starch until they are totally covered, then toss them in the beaten egg.

3. Drop the shrimp in the oil in batches, being careful not to crowd the pan, and cook until they just begin to brown. Remove them with a spider or a slotted spoon to the paper towels.

4. Adjust the heat so that the oil just starts to shimmer again, this time to about 340°F (170°C). Refry all the shrimp until they are golden brown, about 2 minutes more for each batch. Then remove the shrimp to the paper towels and set aside.

5. In a small bowl, combine the soy sauce, oyster sauce, sugar, brown rice syrup, rice wine vinegar, lemon juice, and mirin with 2 tablespoons water and set it aside.

6. In a skillet, heat the olive oil over medium-high heat. Cook the dried chiles, stirring them constantly, for 1 minute.

7. Add the garlic, ginger, onion, and fresh chiles and cook them, stirring constantly, until they are soft, another 4 to 5 minutes.

8. Add the soy sauce mixture to the skillet and let it cook until it thickens, just a few minutes.

9. Add the double-fried shrimp to the skillet and toss until they are just warmed through and coated in the sauce.

10. Serve immediately, garnished with the scallions.

KKONGCHI-JORIM

BRAISED PACIFIC SAURY

This is a very traditional Korean dish, spicy and with a strong flavor of fish oil, though you could tone it down a bit if you made this with a milder, less oily fish like salmon. Pacific saury—the Japanese call it *sanma*; Americans, mackerel pike—is usually bycatch, thus it's very inexpensive. Koreans love it—we even can it. If you can't find it fresh at a Japanese or Korean market, you can use bluefish or mackerel, which, like Pacific saury, is strongly flavored and has skin rather than scales. All can withstand a long braise, which allows the radish slices to soften and soak in that wonderful fish flavor. This is often a main meal with rice, but you can also serve it as *banchan*.

Serves 4 as a main dish

¼ cup (60 ml) soy sauce

2 tablespoons gochugaru

2 tablespoons gochujang

1 tablespoon minced garlic

1 tablespoon minced peeled fresh ginger

1 pound (455 g) Pacific saury, gutted and cleaned (about 2 fish)

2 tablespoons canola oil

1 medium Spanish onion, diced

½ teaspoon kosher salt

1 pound (455 g) Korean moo or daikon radish, peeled, halved, and cut into ½-inch (12 mm) half-moons

1 long green Korean chile, sliced ½ inch (12 mm) thick on the bias

1 Holland chile, sliced ½ inch (12 mm) thick

2 scallions, cut into 2-inch (5 cm) pieces

1   In a small bowl, whisk together the soy sauce, gochugaru, gochujang, garlic, ginger, and 1 cup (240 ml) water. Set aside; this is your sauce.

2   Rinse off the fish and then cut off and discard the heads and tails, if they are still attached. (If there are still little pieces of fin attached, cut them off with scissors.) Cut each fish into 3 roughly equal pieces and set them aside.

3   In a medium saucepan, heat the canola oil over medium heat. Add the onions and salt and cook, stirring frequently, until soft, translucent, and aromatic, about 8 minutes. (Some color is okay, but you don't want them to brown.)

4   Lay the radish slices on top of the onions, then top the radish with the fish pieces. Drizzle the sauce over, cover the pot, and adjust the heat so the sauce is at a simmer. Cook for 20 minutes.

5   Remove the lid, baste the fish with the sauce, and add the chiles and scallions, tucking some of them in between the fish pieces.

6   Let cook for another 15 to 20 minutes, or until the radishes are tender when you pierce them with a fork.

7   Serve hot as a main meal or at room temperature as banchan.

SANGSUN GUI

BROILED BRANZINO

Salted and broiled is the main way Koreans eat all kinds of fish. You score the fish deeply, salt the fish overnight in the refrigerator to dry it out slightly—any fish will do, but I like branzino—then broil it till it sizzles. It's served as the main course of a meal, meant to be shared at the table surrounded by many *banchan*, plus individual bowls of rice for each diner.

Serves 4

1 whole branzino
  (about 1 to
  1½ pounds/
  455 to 680 g)

1½ tablespoons
  kosher salt

1 tablespoon
  grapeseed or
  olive oil

1   Make 3 slits along each side of the fish. Sprinkle the salt over both sides of the fish and let it rest, uncovered, in the refrigerator overnight.

2   The next day, preheat the broiler, and rub the oil over both sides of the fish.

3   Broil the fish, watching it closely, until it starts to brown and sizzle, about 4 to 5 minutes. Flip the fish over and broil the other side until it browns, another 4 to 5 minutes.

4   Serve immediately.

GALCHI GUI

PAN-SEARED SALT-CURED BELT FISH

Another popular traditional dinner in Korea, salt-cured, silvery-skinned belt fish steaks are pan-seared in a little oil and on the table in about five minutes, to accompany rice and *banchan*. It's especially easy because you can find salt-cured belt fish in the refrigerated section of most Asian markets. If you see it, buy extra—it'll last for a long time in the refrigerator.

Serves 4

1 pound (455 g) salted belt fish steaks

1 tablespoon grapeseed or olive oil

1   Rinse the belt fish well under running water, then pat it dry.

2   In a skillet, heat the oil over medium heat. Cook the fish on each side until it is browned and cooked through, about 3 to 4 minutes per side.

3   Serve immediately.

KFC

KOREAN-STYLE FRIED CHICKEN WITH SESAME SEEDS

Korean-style fried chicken has just got that crazy crunch. Dressing it in a spicy-sweet gochujang sauce makes it even more appealing. We tinkered with our batter until we came up with just the right mix: We dredge pre-salted chicken in a dry mix of cornstarch, rice flour, and all-purpose flour, then add a little water to the bowl to make a wet batter for a second coating. The results fry up crisp enough to stand up to the sauce without getting slimy or soggy or becoming a rock-hard shell. One thing about Korean fried chicken is nobody can say their grandmother's is better—it didn't exist in Korea when I was growing up in the 1970s. Instead we had *tongdak*, which means "whole chicken." Vendors would slash the breast and thighs and fry the birds whole, almost rotisserie-style, with no batter at all. You'd take home a whole chicken in a bag, then shred it with your hands to eat as a snack with sweet pickled radish. Today most younger Koreans shrug off what they call *yennal-tongdak* ("old-time whole chicken") for the hot fad of *chi-mek*, aka this recipe served with *mek-ju*, or beer.

Serves 6 to 8

FOR THE CHICKEN
1 whole chicken

Kosher salt

2 quarts (2 L) vegetable oil

1 cup (150 g) rice flour

½ cup (62 g) cornstarch

½ cup (64 g) all-purpose flour

3 cups (700 ml) ice water

FOR THE SAUCE
¼ cup (50 g) turbinado or "raw" sugar

1 cup (240 ml) gochujang

¼ cup (60 ml) soy sauce

2 tablespoons mirin

2 tablespoons fish sauce

2 tablespoons rice wine vinegar

2 tablespoons sesame oil

2 teaspoons minced garlic

FOR SERVING
2 tablespoons toasted sesame seeds

1 thinly sliced scallion, green part only

1 cup (150 g) Dan-Moo (page 175)

1   Using heavy-duty kitchen shears or a sharp knife, cut the chicken into 8 pieces, then cut each breast into 3 roughly even pieces.

2   Sprinkle both sides of all the chicken pieces liberally with the salt and place them in a single layer in a nonreactive container, like a glass baking dish or plastic storage container. Refrigerate the chicken, covered, for at least 6 hours or up to 2 days.

3   Meanwhile, make the sauce: In a medium saucepan, heat the sugar with 2 tablespoons water over medium-low heat, whisking until the sugar has completely dissolved. Remove from the heat and let cool for 5 minutes, then stir in the gochujang, soy sauce, mirin, fish sauce, rice wine vinegar, sesame oil, and garlic. Set this aside while you fry the chicken. (This can be made one day in advance; bring it to room temperature before tossing it with the chicken.)

CONTINUES

4   To fry the chicken: In a heavy-bottomed pot or Dutch oven, heat the vegetable oil over medium heat to 350°F (165°C). Set a wire rack in a baking sheet or line it with paper towels.

5   In a large mixing bowl, combine the rice flour, cornstarch, and all-purpose flour. Dredge the salted chicken pieces in the flour mix so that all sides are covered. Shake off any excess flour and place the chicken pieces in a single layer on a plate or baking sheet.

6   When all the chicken pieces are coated with the flour mixture, make a thin batter by stirring a little bit of the ice water into the flour mixture at a time. Start with 1 cup (240 ml) water and go from there: You want the end result to be the same consistency as crepe batter—thin but not watery.

7   Dip each piece of chicken lightly in the batter, letting the excess drip back into the bowl. (Do this as quickly as you can: You don't want the batter to be too thick or gloppy.) Place the battered pieces back on the plate or baking sheet. The batter may thicken as you go, so adjust with more ice water as needed.

8   To fry the chicken, slowly lower a few pieces into the oil at a time. Don't crowd the pot: You want there to be plenty of room around each piece at all times.

9   Cook the chicken for 6 to 8 minutes, or until an instant-read thermometer inserted into the middle of each piece reads 155°F (68°C). Remove the chicken pieces and let them drain on the rack set in the baking sheet.

10 When all the pieces are fried, add the chicken to a large mixing bowl with ½ cup (120 ml) of the sauce. Toss well until all the chicken pieces are coated, adding more sauce as needed. Sprinkle on the sesame seeds and toss until all pieces are well coated with the seeds.

11 Using tongs, remove the chicken from the bowl to a serving platter. Sprinkle with the sliced scallions and serve with a side of sweet pickled radish.

DAN-MOO

SWEET PICKLED RADISH

A perfect little cube of crunchy sweet radish, and a must if you're serving the KFC (Korean Fried Chicken) on page 172, *dan-moo* is a quick and easy *banchan*. If you have really nice moo with thin, pretty skins, you can skip peeling them and just scrub them well.

You can also turn this into the yellow sweet pickled radish, or *danmuji*, for making the rice rolls called *Kimbop* on page 248, if you're feeling extra DIY. Just cut the radish lengthwise into ½-inch (12 mm) rectangles and add 2 tablespoons of ground turmeric to the vinegar solution.

Serves 8 to 10

2 pounds (910 g) moo radish, peeled and cut into 1-inch (2.5 cm) cubes

4 cups (960 ml) distilled white vinegar

2 cups (400 g) granulated sugar

½ cup (120 g) kosher salt

1   Put the radish cubes in a large glass jar or nonreactive plastic container and set them aside.

2   In a medium saucepan, bring the vinegar, sugar, salt, and 3 cups (720 ml) water to a low simmer, stirring until the sugar dissolves.

3   Let the liquid cool slightly, then pour it over the radishes.

4   Let the jar cool completely, then cover it and store in the refrigerator. These will last for 3 to 4 weeks.

SOONDAE

BLOOD SAUSAGE

This recipe is from Michael Stokes, the chef de cuisine at Insa, who hated that it was so hard to find *soondae*—blood sausage stuffed with glutinous rice and sweet potato noodles—that wasn't dry, over-processed, and mass-produced. You may never make this at home, as it requires several days' worth of steps and a sausage grinder and stuffer in addition to tracking down pork snouts, blood, and sausage casings (just ask your butcher to special order them, or visit the nearest Chinatown). But if you're a maverick project doer/cooking maven, know that this recipe works perfectly. You can slice it into the rice cakes *banchan* on page 262, simmer it in any stew you like, or eat it as a snack. In Korea this is a quintessential market or street food, eaten from a stall and served with toothpicks so you can dip slices into the perilla-seed salt and sesame oil that always accompany this dish.

Makes 10 to 12 sausages

FOR THE PORK SNOUTS

1 pound (450 g) pork snouts, cut into large chunks

¾ cup (150 g) light brown sugar

½ cup (118 ml) soy sauce

1 tablespoon instant coffee

1 small onion, peeled and halved

½ bunch scallions, cut into 2-inch (5 cm) strips

1 dried jujubes (see page 12; optional)

1 tablespoon minced peeled fresh ginger

6 cloves garlic, crushed

1 cinnamon stick

1 star anise pod

2 to 3 whole cloves

FOR THE SAUSAGE GRIND

5 ounces (140 g) pork fat, cut into ½-inch (12 mm) cubes

2 tablespoons minced garlic

2 teaspoons minced peeled fresh ginger

1 tablespoon kosher salt

1 teapoon granulated sugar

2 tablespoons freshly ground black pepper

1 tablespoon gochugaru

1 tablespoon ground toasted sesame seeds

2 bunches coarsely chopped scallions

4 teaspoons sesame oil

4 teaspoons fish sauce

FOR FINISHING THE SAUSAGES

1⅓ cups (275 g) glutinous (sweet) rice, soaked in water for 1 hour and drained

9 ounces (250 ml) sweet potato starch vermicelli

2 cups (450 g) pork blood

Pork sausage casings, soaked, rinsed, and cut into at least ten 12-inch (30.5 cm) lengths

Sesame oil, for serving

FOR THE PERILLA SALT

3 tablespoons perilla seeds

1 tablespoon gochugaru

1 tablespoon salt

½ teaspoon freshly ground black pepper

CONTINUES

1 Cook the pork snouts: Combine everything in a large pot with 4 cups (1 L) water and bring to a boil. Let it cook, covered, for 1 hour, or until the snouts are tender.

2 Let the liquid continue to simmer, but remove the snouts to a bowl and let them cool slightly. While they're still warm, grind them in a meat grinder fitted with the fine plate (or process them in a food processor) and set the meat aside in a bowl.

3 Let the snout cooking liquid reduce until you have about 1 cup (240 ml). Strain the liquid, discarding the solids, and mix the reduced liquid into the ground snouts. Refrigerate the mixture, covered, overnight. This will solidify into a firm, gelatinous block.

4 Prepare the sausage grind: The next day, cut the solidified snout and liquid into ½-inch (12 mm) cubes and combine them in a mixing bowl with the remaining ingredients for the sausage grind. Let the mixture freeze for 30 minutes to 1 hour.

5 While the grind mixture is in the freezer, make the rice and the noodles: Measure the drained rice and put it in a medium pot. Cook rice in boiling water for 4 minutes, then drain. Rinse in cold water until all grains are cold, then drain again.

6 Bring a medium pot of water to a boil and cook the noodles for 4 minutes, then rinse them under running water until they feel cool to the touch. Let them drain completely in a colander in the sink, then roughly chop and set them aside.

7 Use a meat grinder fitted with the fine plate to grind the semi-frozen snout and pork fat mixture, and place the ground meat in a large mixing bowl. Use your hands to add the rice, noodles, and blood until everything is well incorporated. Place the bowl in the refrigerator while you prepare the casings.

8 Make sure there are no large holes in the cleaned casings, and tie them off at one end. (You'll need about 24 pieces of 4-inch/10 cm butcher's twine.) Use a funnel or sausage stuffing machine to loosely stuff each casing about three-quarters full. (Don't pack it too tightly or it may split open when you cook it.) Tie off the other end as you stuff it every 8 inches (20 cm). Retie the casing ½ inch (1.5 cm) down from the original tie so that there is room to cut between each individual link. Prick each sausage 4 or 5 times with a cake tester to let out any air bubbles.

9 Cook the sausages: Put the sausages in a pot with 1 gallon (3.8 L) water and the salt. Bring the pot to a low simmer and cook, uncovered, for about 30 minutes, or until the inside of the sausages is 190–200°F (87–93°C) on an instant-read thermometer or the sausages feel firm to the touch. Prick any sausages that float to the top to release the air. Do not let the pot boil, or the sausages will burst.

10 Remove the sausages from the water and let them cool for about 10 minutes. (At this point, the sausages can be frozen in zip-top bags for up to 3 weeks. Defrost them completely and warm up in a pan or a 350°F/177°C oven before serving.)

11 To make the perilla salt, grind the perilla seeds in a spice mill, then transfer them to a small mixing bowl.

12 Whisk in the gochugaru, the salt, and the pepper. (This will keep for several weeks in an airtight container.)

13 Serve the sausages immediately, cut into thick slices, with the perilla salt and sesame oil on the side.

CHICKEN CUTLETS
À LA DONKATSU

Koreans adopted the fast-food favorite *donkatsu* from the Japanese. It's typically made with pork that is pounded ultra-thin, seasoned, breaded, and deep-fried, but I make mine with chicken. I skip the pounding—I don't think it needs it, but you can make them even thinner if you like—and I pan-fry it in a little less oil. You can serve these cutlets as *banchan* or as a full meal with rice, a little shredded fresh cabbage, or kimchi. My kids, who prefer ketchup as their dipping sauce, call this dish Mom's Chicken Fingers and help me make it at least once a week. I prefer to slather mine with sriracha blended with ketchup and Worcestershire sauce. You can use whatever you like from your fridge. Leftovers, if there are any, make for great sandwiches.

Serves 4

2 boneless, skinless chicken breasts (about 1½ pounds/680 g)

1½ teaspoons kosher salt

Freshly ground black pepper

⅓ cup (40 g) all-purpose flour

2 large eggs, beaten

1 cup (25 g) panko breadcrumbs

¼ cup (60 ml) grapeseed or olive oil

1 cup (95 g) finely shredded green cabbage

Basic Jap Gok Bop (Healthy Rice, page 260)

1   Cut each breast horizontally into thirds, so you end up with 6 pieces.

2   Season the chicken pieces with salt and pepper on both sides.

3   Set up three bowls for the coating: one with the flour, one with the beaten eggs, and one with the panko.

4   Dip each piece of chicken into the flour first, dusting off any excess; then into the eggs, making sure it is coated completely; and finally into the panko, making sure the whole piece is evenly coated. Let the coated chicken pieces rest on a plate for at least 15 minutes and up to 30.

5   In a large skillet, heat the oil over medium-high heat. Once the oil is shimmering, add the breaded chicken pieces to the pan without crowding them. (You may need to do this in batches.)

6   Cook the chicken until the bottom is golden brown, about 2 to 3 minutes. Flip the pieces over and let the other side brown, about 2 to 3 minutes more.

7   Remove the pieces to paper towels and let them rest for 10 minutes. Cut them into long, thick strips and serve them with cabbage, rice, and whatever condiments you prefer for dipping.

YUKHWE

KOREAN STEAK TARTARE

Yukhwe—pronounced "YOOK-hway"—is the Korean version of steak tartare, though the traditional version is cut into long, skinny, stringier pieces, more like a rough julienne, rather than a steak tartare's fine chop. I prefer the texture of small cubes in the French method of making tartare, but you can julienne yours if you prefer. The Asian pear is traditional, and some recipes call for pine nuts, though I like the tangy pop of fried capers. My father loved this dish when I was growing up, and in Korea you'd go out for this as a main meal, with white rice and soup. (I love it now, too, but I have to admit as a little kid I thought yukhwe, the only Korean dish I know of where red meat is served raw, was gross.) This is so easy to make—the key is just using the best-quality steak you can find. You want it to be on the leaner side, which is why I call for eye round, and you also want it to be very fresh, not aged. In Korea some restaurants even hang up signs advertising their "new beef" yukhwe, letting you know the meat is only a day or two old. To that end you'll want to eat this as soon as you make it, and don't worry about storing leftovers safely: Trust me, you won't have any! Serve it with Bugak, or any kind of cracker, grilled bread, or potato chip.

Serves 2

½ pound (225 g) eye round steak

2 tablespoons olive oil

1 tablespoon capers

½ cup (60 g) finely diced Asian pear

1 scallion, minced

1½ tablespoons white soy sauce (see Note, page 92)

⅛ teaspoon freshly ground black pepper, plus more to taste

2 tablespoons sesame oil

⅛ teaspoon kosher salt, plus more to taste

1 extra-large egg yolk

Bugak (Crispy Fried Seaweed Chips, page 58), for serving

1   Place the steak in the freezer for 1 hour.

2   Meanwhile, in the smallest saucepan you have, heat the olive oil over medium-high heat. Add the capers and let them fry until they are crispy, about 3 minutes. Use a slotted spoon or strainer to drain on paper towels.

3   Cut the steak into small cubes. Add the cubes to a large mixing bowl with the fried capers, pear, scallion, soy sauce, black pepper, sesame oil, and salt. Mix well and taste for salt and pepper.

4   Transfer the beef mixture to a serving bowl. Place the egg yolk at the center of the bowl, atop the beef mixture, then sprinkle additional black pepper over the yolk. Serve immediately, while everything is still cold, and mix in the yolk and the beef together at the table. Serve crispy fried seaweed chips on the side.

BULGOGI

GRILLED SIRLOIN

Growing up in Korea in the seventies, we had "fire beef" (*bul* means "fire" and *gogi* means "meat") for very special occasions. Though this is pretty much everyone's favorite type of Korean BBQ, and one of the few Korean things even non-Koreans know, I have to admit that when the pile of bulgogi appeared on the table, I mainly wanted the extra drippings in the bottom of the pan so that I could drown my rice in it, topping the bowl with a piece of kimchi. The sweetness of the meat and that sauce combined with fermented cabbage is a flavor combination made in heaven. This is one BBQ that may benefit from being cooked on the stovetop, rather than a grill: On a grill, you lose the sauce to the fire! My perfect bulgogi bite is with rice, *ssam jang*, and grilled onions on a piece of red leaf lettuce with a perilla leaf. Add a soup, and you'll have a complete Korean meal.

Serves 6 to 8

FOR THE BULGOGI

1 cup (240 ml) soy sauce

⅔ cup (135 g) granulated sugar

⅔ cup (85 g) grated onion

⅔ cup (170 g) grated Asian pear

2 tablespoons minced garlic

2 tablespoons sesame oil

2 teaspoons minced peeled fresh ginger

2 teaspoons freshly ground black pepper

4 pounds (1.8 kg) sirloin, sliced as thinly as possible against the grain

Canola oil, for greasing

1 medium onion, thinly sliced lengthwise

1 bunch scallions, cut into 2-inch (5 cm) strips

FOR SERVING

Lettuces and Herbs (page 157)

Ssam Jang (page 157)

2 to 3 Banchan (see pages 16–131)

Rice (page 15)

1. Make the bulgogi: In a zip-top bag or nonreactive storage container, mix together the soy sauce, sugar, onion, pear, garlic, sesame oil, ginger, and black pepper. Add the sliced sirloin and marinate it for at least 30 minutes at room temperature or up to overnight in the refrigerator.

2. Heat a skillet or grill pan over high heat. Coat the bottom with a little oil, just enough so the beef won't stick, then add the meat in a single layer without crowding the pan; you don't want the meat to steam. (You may need to do this in batches.)

3. Cook the meat until it is charred on one side, about 2 to 3 minutes. Then flip and cook it to your desired degree of doneness—about 1 minute more for rare, 2 to 3 minutes more for medium or well-done. (Koreans prefer it well-done.)

4. When the meat is done, set it aside on a serving platter and add the onions and scallions to the pan. Cook until they are soft and translucent, about 3 minutes, then add them to the serving platter.

5. Serve immediately with the lettuces and herbs, ssam jang, banchan, and rice.

YANG KALBI

SPICED LAMB RIBS

This is a famous northern Chinese dish that the chef de cuisine of Insa, Michael Stokes, adapted to Korean flavors for the restaurant, where we serve it as a shared plate. The key is the cure and then the slow cooking. At Insa—and traditionally at Chinese restaurants—the lamb ribs are deep-fried before being brushed with spicy-sweet sauce and sprinkled with a wonderful cumin-coriander-chile spice mix, but they are just as good without the bath in the deep fryer.

NOTE: Be careful not to confuse lamb ribs with rack of lamb: They are two very different cuts—luckily, the lamb ribs are both more affordable, and, in my opinion, more delicious.

Serves 4

1 rack (about 2 pounds/910 g) lamb ribs (see Note)

¼ cup (60 ml) shaoxing Chinese rice cooking wine

5 teaspoons kosher salt

2 scallions

7 cloves garlic, 2 whole and 5 minced

2 tablespoons grapeseed or olive oil

1 yellow onion, minced

2 tablespoons minced peeled fresh ginger

⅓ cup (80 g) gochujang

¼ cup (60 ml) rice wine vinegar

2 tablespoons soy sauce

2 tablespoons packed brown sugar

1 tablespoon honey

1 tablespoon whole cumin seeds

1 tablespoon whole coriander seeds

1 tablespoon whole perilla seeds

1 tablespoon toasted sesame seeds

2 tablespoons gochugaru

½ teaspoon mustard powder

½ teaspoon garlic powder

¼ teaspoon freshly ground black pepper

2 tablespoons granulated sugar

1   In a nonreactive baking dish, coat the ribs with the cooking wine and then sprinkle 3 teaspoons of the salt evenly over both sides. Let them rest, covered, in the refrigerator overnight.

2   The next day, preheat the oven to 250°F (120°C). Tightly double-wrap the ribs, scallions, and the whole and minced garlic cloves in heavy-duty aluminum foil and place the packet on a baking sheet.

3   Cook until the ribs are tender, about 2 to 2½ hours.

4   While the ribs are cooking, in a skillet, heat the oil over medium heat. Cook the onions and ginger until very soft and caramelized, about 10 to 12 minutes.

5   Add the gochujang, vinegar, soy sauce, brown sugar, and honey and let it just come to a simmer. Turn off the heat and set the sauce aside.

6   In a dry skillet over medium heat, separately toast the cumin, coriander, perilla, and sesame seeds, if they are not already toasted.

7   Grind the toasted seeds with a mortar and pestle or a spice mill, until they are coarsely ground but still with some whole pieces. In a small mixing bowl, blend together the ground seeds with the remaining 2 teaspoons of salt, gochugaru, mustard powder, garlic powder, black pepper, and granulated sugar. Set the spice blend aside in a shallow bowl or plate.

8   When the lamb ribs are done, let them rest for 10 minutes, then separate the ribs by cutting along each bone.

9   Generously brush the sauce over the ribs, then dip each one in the spice mix. Serve immediately, with any kind of kimchi or pickles, if desired.

SPAM

After the Korean War, the U.S. government handed out food to South Koreans, including loads of canned Spam. It was our first introduction to salty, fatty, umami-filled potted meat, and we embraced it. You can use it in stews, Bibimbop (page 246), and Kimchi Fried Rice (page 258), or just pan-fry cubes of it and serve it as *banchan*. This recipe is from Michael Stokes, the chef de cuisine at Insa.

NOTE: Curing salt, also known as pink salt, is a mix of table salt and sodium nitrite used in the meat-curing process to prohibit the growth of certain bacteria and enhance the flavor of the meat. It's usually dyed pink to distinguish it from regular salt.

Makes 1 (5½ by 10½-inch (14 by 27 cm) loaf

10 ounces (280 g) pork skin, cut into strips

2 pounds (900 g) pork butt or shoulder

1.3 pounds (590 g) pork fat

¾ pound (350 g) bacon

1 tablespoon minced garlic

1 tablespoon granulated sugar

2 tablespoons kosher salt

1 teaspoon curing salt #1 (see Note)

3 ounces (90 g) potato starch or cornstarch

9 ounces (250 g) ice

1   In a small pot, cover the pork skin with 2 inches (5 cm) water. Bring to a boil, then simmer over medium heat for 1 hour. Drain the strips and discard the liquid, then refrigerate the strips until they have cooled completely.

2   Preheat the oven to 250°F (120°C).

3   Cut the pork butt, pork fat, and bacon into 1-inch (2.5 cm) pieces. Combine them in a large mixing bowl with the cooled pork skin and the remaining ingredients. Toss until everything is well combined.

4   Pass everything through a meat grinder fitted with the fine plate, then process half of this mixture in a food processor until it is a smooth puree. In a large mixing bowl, fold the puree back into the ground meat mixture and stir until it is well combined.

5   Line a large 5½ by 10½-inch (14 by 27 cm) loaf pan with plastic wrap so that the wrap overlaps the sides, and fill it with the meat mixture, making sure there are no air pockets.

6   Fold the ends of the plastic over the top, and then wrap the loaf pan completely in aluminum foil.

7   Place the loaf pan in a deep baking dish, then pour water into the baking dish so it reaches halfway up the sides of the loaf pan, and bake until the internal temperature of the meat mixture reaches 150°F (65°C), about 3 to 4 hours,

8   Remove the loaf pan from the oven and let it cool for 30 minutes, then remove the foil and drain off any excess liquid.

9   Place the loaf pan in a baking dish, then place a second loaf pan on top of the first one, filling it with about 10 pounds (4.5 kg) of weight. Let the Spam chill overnight in the refrigerator under the weight—the baking dish will catch any drips.

10   The next day, remove the weight and top loaf pan. Place the loaf pan with the Spam in a baking dish filled with hot water for about a minute to loosen the meat.

11   Turn the Spam out onto a plate or baking sheet and remove the plastic wrap. Cut the Spam into portions and serve immediately, refrigerate for 2 to 3 days, or freeze for up to 2 months.

After *hanchan*, soups (*guk*) and stews (*jjigae*) are the most Korean things of all—they are what we really eat on a day-to-day basis. We use the words *jjim* and *tang* for these things as well: They once had specific meanings, but now they blur together. A meal of rice and soup or rice and stew for a Korean is like a sandwich is to an American. These dishes can be both homey, as in what you fix for yourself for dinner, or celebratory, as in the thing you order at a fancy restaurant and share for a special occasion. Koreans love them, and they crave them, and I think it's one thing that sets Korea's cuisine apart from the cooking of Japan or China.

For Koreans, boiling is a respected technique: We don't usually make a stock before we make soup, we just boil it all together. In fact, the Korean cooking lexicon includes the word *bahgul bahgul*, for the sound the pot makes when it is at a boil. And we have a whole set of fancy clay pots for soups and stews, *ttkekhaegi*, that go from stove to table.

Soups and stews are also very seasonal, and many have their own traditions: Samgae Tang (page 214), rice-stuffed chicken soup, for example, is eaten in the hottest part of the summer, because we believe that it helps to fight fire with fire and beat the humid weather. Tteok Guk (page 194), or rice cake soup, is often embellished with the dumplings called *mandu* and eaten on New Year's Day to mark getting older and wiser. Miyeok Guk (page 198) is for birthdays, and Seolleon Tang (page 226) is for when you're hungover or feeling weak or sick. Many are deeply rooted in tradition, each one helping to mark the passing of a year.

GUK, JJIGAE, JJIM & TANG
SOUPS & STEWS

SOGOGI MOO GUK

RADISH AND BEEF SOUP

So very simple and so very good on chilly gray days. Most Koreans just throw all the ingredients into a pot, but I borrow a trick from the Western world and brown the meat a little bit in the sesame oil first. Next to the seaweed soup on page 198, this is one of the most comforting dishes I know. My grandmother used to use beef scraps in this peasant dish, but I like brisket—and we made it really luxurious by using a pound of meat!

Serves 6 to 8

1 pound (455 g) beef brisket, chuck, sirloin, or eye round

1 teaspoon sesame oil

1 teaspoon grapeseed or olive oil

1 tablespoon minced garlic

Kosher salt

1½ pounds (680 g) moo radish, peeled, quartered, and cut into ¼-inch (6 mm) half-moon slices

4 scallions, cut into 2-inch (5 cm) pieces

1½ teaspoons fish sauce

Freshly ground black pepper

1. Trim off as much fat as you can from the beef (this keeps the soup from becoming too oily) and cut the meat into 2 pieces.

2. In a large saucepan or stockpot, heat the sesame and grapeseed oils over medium-high heat. Sear the brisket until both sides are slightly browned, about 3 or 4 minutes per side.

3. Add the garlic, 12 cups (2.8 L) water, and 1 teaspoon salt, then increase the heat to medium-high and bring everything to a boil. Reduce the heat to medium and let simmer for 20 minutes.

4. Add the radish and simmer for another 30 minutes.

5. Remove the meat to a cutting board and let it rest until it is cool enough to handle.

6. Meanwhile, add the scallions, 1½ teaspoons salt, and the fish sauce to the broth.

7. Slice the beef as thin as you can and return it to the pot, then serve immediately, sprinkled with a little black pepper.

TTEOK-MANDU GUK

RICE CAKE AND DUMPLING SOUP

This simple, restorative rice cake soup, graced with thin wedges of fresh radish and a light beef broth, is eaten all year long, but it is always served on New Year's Day, along with tangerines, noodles, fritters, and other good-luck holiday dishes. Like many Koreans, I like to put a few homemade *mandu*, or dumplings, into the pot. Other ways to gild the lily include garnishes like thin ribbons of cooked omelet, crushed roasted seaweed, or a few beautiful red strands of shilgochu, or Korean chile threads. They look like saffron and provide a similar spike of flavor once they soak in the broth.

NOTE: Don't leave the rice cakes in the broth for more than 20 minutes before serving the soup, or they will soak up all the broth; dumplings also tend to get soggy when left to soak too long. I like to make this soup even more substantial by adding a bit of the milky broth from Seollong Tang on page 226.

Serves 4 to 6

FOR THE SOUP

¾ pound (340 g) beef brisket, chuck, sirloin, or eye round

1 teaspoon sesame oil

1 teaspoon olive oil

1 tablespoon minced garlic

Kosher salt

½ pound (225 g) moo or daikon radish, peeled, quartered, and cut into ½-inch (12 mm) slices

4 scallions, cut lengthwise into 1-inch (2.5 cm) pieces

2 teaspoons fish sauce

12 fresh or frozen mandu (see pages 266 and 269)

¾ cup (170 g) sliced rice cakes, fresh or frozen (see page 262)

Freshly ground black pepper

Soy sauce

FOR SERVING (OPTIONAL)

1 large egg, lightly beaten

Roasted seaweed (see page 13), thinly sliced

Thinly sliced scallions

Shilgochu (Korean chile threads)

1 Make the soup: Trim off as much fat as you can from the beef and cut the meat into 3 pieces.

2 In a large saucepan or stockpot, heat the sesame and olive oils over medium-high heat. Sear the brisket until both sides are slightly browned, about 3 or 4 minutes per side.

3 Add the garlic, 1 gallon (3.8 L) water, and 1 teaspoon salt, then bring everything to a boil. Reduce the heat to medium and let simmer for 35 minutes. Skim impurities as they rise to the surface.

4 Add the radish and let the soup simmer for another 30 minutes, until the meat is tender.

5 Remove the meat to a cutting board and let it rest until it is cool enough to handle.

6 Meanwhile, add the scallions, 1½ teaspoons salt, the fish sauce, and the mandu to the soup.

7 Slice the beef as thinly as you can and return it to the pot. Add the sliced rice cakes and let them cook for 5 minutes, or until they are soft. Season to taste with black pepper and soy sauce.

8 To serve, stir the egg into the pot, If using, letting it cook for a few seconds.

9 Serve immediately with the optional seaweed, scallions, and chile threads as desired.

YUKGAEJANG

SPICY BEEF SOUP

In Korea, this is a very popular soup with taxi drivers and truck drivers, who stop for it at small roadside dives. My mother makes a really good version, but it turns out that she, like most cooks, finishes the soup with a bit of powdered stock or the flavor booster MSG. This version is pure and simple and from-scratch, and tastes just as good, minus the MSG—not that there's anything wrong with a little MSG. This is meant to be eaten as a meal with a bowl of rice and *banchan*, including at least one kimchi.

Serves 4 to 6

- 1 tablespoon grapeseed or olive oil
- 1¼ pounds (570 g) flank steak
- ½ white onion, diced
- 5 dried anchovies, head and guts removed
- 3 cloves garlic, smashed
- 1½ cups (35 g) dried bracken, soaked in warm water for 1 hour
- 1 bunch spring onions or 2 bunches large scallions, cut into 2-inch (5 cm) strips
- 1 leek, light green and white parts only, cut into 2-inch (5 cm) strips
- 2 tablespoons minced garlic
- 5 tablespoons (40 g) gochugaru
- 2 tablespoons sesame oil
- 1 tablespoon fish sauce
- 2 tablespoons soy sauce
- 1 tablespoon kosher salt
- 1 teaspoon freshly ground black pepper
- 2 large eggs
- 1 cup cooked *dangmyeon* noodles

1. In a large pot, heat the grapeseed oil over medium-high heat. Sear the flank steak on all sides until it is well browned, about 8 to 10 minutes.

2. Add 1 gallon (3.8 L) water to the pot and the onion, anchovies, and smashed garlic. Bring the pot to a boil, then reduce the heat so it cooks at a simmer for 1 hour.

3. Drain and rinse the bracken and cut it into 2-inch (5 cm) strips. Add the strips to a small bowl with the scallions, leek, minced garlic, gochugaru, sesame oil, fish sauce, soy sauce, salt, and black pepper. Toss everything together and set aside.

4. Remove the flank steak from the stock and set it aside to rest for 30 minutes. Strain the solids from the stock and discard them.

5. Add the bracken mixture to the stock and let it cook at a low simmer for 30 minutes.

6. Slice the rested steak against the grain and add it to the pot, then gently crack the eggs into the soup, breaking them up with a fork so they loosely scramble in the liquid.

7. Add the cooked noodles and taste for salt. Serve immediately.

MIYEOK GUK

SEAWEED SOUP

This is one of my all-time favorite soups. I make a big batch and eat it all week to celebrate a birthday or to ward off a cold. The seaweed is filled with great umami flavor, plus it has such a soft, supple texture. For this dish, look for the words *ito-wakame* or *wakame* on the seaweed package. (They are Japanese terms, and the Korean variety always comes with quotation marks around these words.) It is very important to soak it in warm water for at least 10 minutes before you use it, to soften it. You can also make this soup without the beef—add a little more soy sauce or fish sauce and it will be just as delicious.

Serves 4 to 6

2 tablespoons extra-virgin olive oil

½ pound (225 g) beef chuck, cut into thin slices

10 cloves garlic, minced

1 ounce (28 g) dried seaweed or wakame seaweed, thinly sliced and soaked in warm water

2 tablespoons sesame oil

1 teaspoon fish sauce

2 teaspoons soy sauce

2 teaspoons kosher salt

5 dried anchovies, heads and guts removed

1 teaspoon freshly ground black pepper

3 scallions, thinly sliced

1 tablespoons toasted sesame seeds

1   In a large, heavy-bottomed pot, heat the olive oil over high heat. Sear the beef until it is well browned and crusted on all sides, 5 to 7 minutes.

2   Add the garlic and sauté until it is fragrant, about 1½ minutes.

3   Reduce the heat to medium-high. Drain the seaweed and add it to the pot along with the sesame oil. Cook for about 3 minutes, then add 12 cups (2.8 L) water and the fish sauce, soy sauce, salt, anchovies, and black pepper.

4   Bring to a boil and simmer until the meat is tender, about 1 hour. Season to taste with more fish sauce, soy sauce, or salt.

5   Garnish with scallions and sesame seeds and serve hot.

BUGEO GUK

EGG AND DRIED FISH SOUP

This is a mild soup, like an egg drop soup, made with the dried fish called *bugeo*, or pollack, that Korean cooks keep on hand in the pantry. It is not at all fishy—it has a little bit of the taste of the sea, but is mainly just comforting. Some might say it's a bit bland, but I really love the subtle flavor and texture of the dried fish in this simple and humble soup.

NOTE: To shred the dried fish, use your fingers to tear it into long, bite-size threads, combing through it to make sure there aren't any bones the same way you'd pick through crabmeat. I keep the skin on, as that's where much of those good omega-3s reside.

Serves 6 to 8

2 tablespoons sesame oil

3 ounces (85 g) dried and shredded pollack (see Note)

1 pound (455 g) moo radish, peeled, quartered, and sliced into ¼-inch (6 mm) half-moons

2 teaspoons minced garlic

3 teaspoons kosher salt

2 teaspoons fish sauce

1 teaspoon soy sauce

3 large eggs, beaten

5 scallions, sliced into 2-inch (5 cm) pieces

¼ teaspoon freshly ground black pepper

1 In a large stockpot, heat the oil over medium heat. Stir-fry the pollack until fragrant, about 1 minute.

2 Add the moo radish, garlic, 1 teaspoon of the salt, and 14 cups (3.3 L) water.

3 Raise the heat to high and bring to a boil. Skim impurities as they rise to the surface, then lower the heat to maintain a simmer. Cook for 20 minutes, or until the radish is tender.

4 Stir in the remaining 2 teaspoons salt, fish sauce, and the soy sauce, adding more of all three to taste as desired.

5 Stir in the eggs and scallions. Let them cook for 1 minute, then turn off the heat.

6 Stir in the black pepper and serve hot.

SOONDUBU

SILKEN TOFU STEW WITH SEAFOOD

This is one of the best uses of silken tofu ever and one of my favorite Korean stews: It's creamy, slightly spicy, and thoroughly satisfying. In any city with a Koreatown, you'll find at least one restaurant that specializes only in *soondubu*, with soft pillows of tofu in a slightly spicy, savory broth, supplemented with beef, pork, chicken, or seafood, which to me is the classic variation. If you can find freshly made silken tofu, by all means use it, otherwise just use the best quality you can find. Same goes for the seafood, and try not to limit yourself to just one kind—a mix of shrimp, squid, cleaned clams, and mussels will add another dimension to your soondubu.

NOTE: You want to use the smallest pot that will fit the ingredients for this soup, not a large stockpot, as you don't want the liquid to evaporate. Traditionally, this dish is made in a round Korean *ttukbaegi*, a clay pot that holds heat and goes from stove to table. Also take care not to stir the soup too aggressively as it simmers: You want the tofu to stay as intact as possible.

Serves 2 to 4

1 tablespoon grapeseed or olive oil

¼ medium white onion, diced

2 scallions, thinly sliced, whites and greens separated

2 teaspoons minced garlic

⅓ cup (70 g) chopped Baechu Kimchi (page 102)

2 tablespoons gochugaru

2 tablespoons soy sauce

1 tablespoon fish sauce

1 cup Master Anchovy Stock (page 228)

8 to 9 ounces (225 to 255 g) silken tofu

½ cup (3 ounces/75 g) raw shrimp

½ cup (3.5 ounces/ 100 g) raw squid, cut into rings

3 to 5 cleaned clams or mussels

Kosher salt

1 large egg, (optional)

½ cup (60 g) fresh watercress, thick stems removed (optional)

1   In a small pot (see Note), heat the oil over medium-high heat. Add the onion, whites of the scallions, and the garlic and cook, stirring occasionally, until soft, about 5 to 7 minutes. Do not let them burn.

2   Stir in the kimchi and let it heat through.

3   Add the gochugaru, soy sauce, fish sauce, and anchovy stock. Increase the heat and bring everything to a simmer.

4   Add the tofu and the seafood. Increase the heat so everything cooks at a low boil, then let it cook until the seafood is just opaque or the shells open, about 3 to 4 minutes. With a wooden spoon or spatula, stir to make sure nothing is sticking to the bottom or sides of the pot. (Don't stir the tofu too much, or it will break apart.) Check for seasoning, and adjust with salt, soy sauce, or fish sauce as needed.

5   If desired, crack the egg into the pot and top the pot with the watercress. Sprinkle the green part of the scallions over the top and serve immediately.

SEE HOW-TO ON FOLLOWING PAGES

1 Before you add the kimchi, cook the onions and garlic until they are very soft—a little brown is okay, but don't let them burn. This is not traditional—for most stews, Koreans generally throw everything into a clay pot and bring it to a hard boil. Years of cooking professionally have taught me that when you slowly cook vegetables, or sweat them, it brings out their sweetness, meaning that unlike with many modern *soondubu* recipes, you don't have to add sugar.

2 Instead of a meat stock or broth, the gochugaru, soy sauce, fish sauce, gochujang, and anchovy stock are the flavor building blocks for this stew. Once they're in the pot, increase the heat and let everything come to a simmer to let those flavors meld.

3 Be very gentle with the silken tofu; do not stir the stew too much as you prepare it. When you eat the soup, you don't want little pieces or shreds of tofu—you want big, creamy spoonfuls.

4 Most Korean home cooks and restaurants just buy a bag of mixed cooked frozen seafood, which you can get in Korean markets, but this stew tastes so much better with fresh product. I prefer to leave a little bit of the tail on my shrimp, just for looks, but you don't have to.

KIMCHI JJIGAE

KIMCHI STEW

On a traditional Korean table, there's always a stew or a soup of some kind, along with myriad *banchan*, kimchi, and, of course, plain steamed rice. In my house, we always had either this or the Doenjang Jjigae on the next page, though this is far better known in the States. Take your pick, as both are delicious, and be sure to serve both with plenty of hot rice.

Serves 2 to 4

6 ounces (175 g) pork belly, diced

1 cup (125 g) diced onion

2 cups (300 g) chopped Baechu Kimchi (page 102)

3 cups (720 ml) Master Anchovy Stock (page 228) or water

2 tablespoons gochugaru

1 tablespoon gochujang

2 scallions, cut into 2-inch (5 cm) pieces

½ pound (225 g) firm tofu, cut into 1-inch (2.5 cm) cubes

1   Heat a medium stockpot over medium heat. Cook the pork belly until it is cooked through but not crispy, or it will taste rubbery and dry in the stew. Remove most of the rendered fat, leaving about 1 tablespoon of it in the pot.

2   Add the onion and kimchi and sauté until the onions are soft and translucent, 5 to 8 minutes.

3   Add the stock, gochugaru, and gochujang. Bring everything to a boil and simmer for 30 minutes.

4   Add the scallions and tofu and cook for 10 minutes more, until they are heated through. Serve immediately.

DOENJANG JJIGAE

SOYBEAN PASTE STEW

Filled with squash, potatoes, fresh and dried chiles, and tofu, this stew is a familiar sight on any Korean dinner table. Like Kimchi Jjigae (page 206), it's simple, affordable, flavorful, and healthy. This is one stew where I really think it tastes best prepared in a *ttukbaegi*, or traditional Korean clay pot. It's just the right size for letting the water reduce to exactly the right proportions. You can serve it in the center of the table with a ladle and small individual soup bowls.

Serves 4

⅓ cup (75 ml) doenjang

7 dried anchovies, head and guts removed and tied in cheesecloth or placed in a tea ball

1 small potato, cut into ¾-inch (2 cm) cubes

½ pound (225 g) squash or zucchini, cut lengthwise and sliced into ½-inch (12 mm) half-moons

½ pound (225 g) firm tofu, cut into 1-inch (2.5 cm) cubes

1 cup (125 g) diced white onion

1 whole Korean green chile, seeded and thinly sliced ½ inch thick

1 whole Holland chile, seeded and thinly sliced ½ inch thick

½ teaspoon gochugaru

1 tablespoon minced garlic

2 scallions, cut into 2-inch (5 cm) pieces, white and green parts separated

Kosher salt

1 In a small mixing bowl, whisk the doenjang into 1 cup (240 ml) water.

2 Strain the doenjang mixture through a sieve into a medium saucepot. Add 4 cups (960 ml) water, the anchovies, and the potatoes and heat over medium heat. Let cook for about 10 minutes at a low simmer.

3 Add the squash, tofu, and onion to the pot, and let it cook at a simmer for another 7 or 8 minutes.

4 Add the chiles, gochugaru, garlic, and white parts of the scallions to pot. Let it cook at a simmer for another 10 minutes.

5 Taste the soup for seasoning, adding salt as necessary, and garnish with the scallion greens.

KKOTGAE TANG

CRAB STEW

This super-delicious crab soup can be made with any white-fleshed fish, large shrimp, clams, or mussels. With crabs, be sure to get all the meat out of the shells with a pair of sharp chopsticks and some kitchen shears.

NOTE: You can either clean fresh crabs yourself, or use a bag of flash-frozen crabs, sold at Asian supermarkets (see page 164).

Serves 4

½ cup (30 g) sliced white onion

1 tablespoon minced garlic

1 cup (200 g) thinly sliced moo radish

3 large dried anchovies, heads and guts removed

2 tablespoons doenjang

2 pounds (910 g) cleaned blue crabs (see Note)

2 tablespoons gochujang

2 teaspoons gochugaru

3 scallions, cut into 2-inch (5 cm) pieces

1 jalapeño, thinly sliced

1 small zucchini, halved lengthwise and sliced into thin half-moons

1   Put the onion, garlic, and radish in a medium saucepot with 5 cups (1.2 L) water and bring it to a boil, then reduce the heat so the pot cooks at a simmer.

2   Tie the anchovies and doenjang in a cheesecloth (to strain out the soybeans) and place it in the pot.

3   Add the crabs, gochujang, and gochugaru and let them simmer for 10 minutes.

4   Add the scallions, jalapeño, and zucchini and cook the soup for another 5 to 7 minutes, then serve immediately.

DAKDORI TANG

SPICY CHICKEN STEW

A classic one-pot meal that's great for a weeknight, this is a dish I used to make a lot when I was younger and dirt-poor. After years of searing chicken or browning meat before making a stew, now I often embrace the Korean method of boiling everything in the pot together, though in the summer, I grill a few chicken pieces and toss them into the sauce to braise for about 30 minutes.

Serves 6 to 8

¼ cup (60 ml)
soy sauce

2 tablespoons
minced peeled
fresh ginger

8 cloves garlic,
minced

¼ cup (60 g)
gochujang

3 tablespoons
gochugaru

1 tablespoon
fish sauce

1 tablespoon
granulated sugar

1 whole chicken,
cut into 8 pieces

2 medium Yukon
gold potatoes,
or whole baby
potatoes, diced

1 cup (140 g) cubed
moo radish

2 Korean green
chiles, sliced
¼ inch (6 mm)
thick

1 bunch scallions,
white parts only,
cut into 2-inch
(5 cm) pieces

1   Make a seasoning paste by mixing the soy sauce, ginger, garlic, gochujang, gochugaru, fish sauce, and sugar in a small bowl.

2   In a medium saucepot, combine the chicken with the seasoning paste and 3 cups (720 ml) water. Bring the pot to a boil, cover the pot, then reduce the heat so it cooks at a simmer for 15 minutes.

3   Add the potatoes and radish and cook for another 15 minutes, covered, on low heat. Add more water if the pot looks dry.

4   Stir in the green chiles and scallions. Let everything cook for another 5 to 10 minutes, uncovered, until the sauce thickens slightly. Serve immediately.

SAMGAE TANG

RICE-STUFFED CORNISH GAME HEN IN SOUP

Ironically, Koreans love to eat this cure-all tonic piping hot on the hottest days of summer! I ate one of the best *samgae tang* I've ever had on a hot July afternoon in Seoul, where people lined up out the door to consume an entire bowl of stuffed chicken in double-strength chicken stock. It was served simply with perfectly made kimchi and seasoned soy sauce on the side—my mind was blown.

NOTE: Ginseng root is available at Asian markets, but burdock or parsnip roots are good substitutes in a pinch.

Serves 1

½ cup (90 g) glutinous (sweet) rice

Kosher salt

1 Cornish game hen, patted dry

7 cloves garlic

2 tablespoons minced peeled fresh ginger

3 dried jujubes (see page 12)

1 large ginseng root (see Note)

4 to 5 cups (960 ml to 1.2 L) chicken stock

1 scallion, thinly sliced, for garnish

Freshly ground black pepper, for garnish

Baechu Kimchi (page 102), for serving

Soy sauce, for serving

1   Soak the sweet rice in 2 cups (480 ml) water and let sit for 1 hour, then strain the water from the rice, leaving the rice to sit in the strainer for 10 minutes, shaking off excess water.

2   Sprinkle salt liberally on all sides of the game hen and let it sit at room temperature for 1 hour.

3   In a small bowl, mix together the drained rice with the garlic, ginger, and jujubes, then stuff it into the cavity of the salted hen.

4   Put the hen in a pot with the ginseng and cover it with the chicken stock.

5   Bring the pot to a boil, then lower the heat, cover the pot, and let it cook at a simmer for about 45 minutes.

6   Serve the chicken in the broth, garnished with the scallions and sprinkled with black pepper; serve the kimchi and soy sauce on the side. Serve immediately, generally one Cornish game hen per person.

KALBI TANG
SHORT RIB SOUP

This is a luxurious beef and noodle soup that is embellished with a spoonful of chunky ginger-soy-chile-scallion yangnyum sauce. It's wonderful on cold winter days. The noodles are springy *dangmyeon*, sometimes labeled sweet potato noodles or Korean vermicelli, which stand up to long cooking. This soup begins with the traditional method of making a clear broth by cleaning and soaking the bones to remove some of the blood before they are simmered. I also like to stir a little kimchi juice into my bowl of soup, but that's just me.

Serves 6 to 8

FOR THE SOUP

3 to 4 pounds (1.4 to 1.8 kg) bone-in short ribs, trimmed of extra fat

Kosher salt

1 medium onion, halved

2 scallions

10 cloves garlic

2 thick slices fresh ginger

1 pound (455 g) moo radish cut into thin quarters

2 teaspoons soy sauce

1 teaspoon fish sauce (optional)

3 ounces (85 g) dangmyeon noodles

¼ teaspoon freshly ground black pepper

Egg ribbons (see step 9, page 238), thinly sliced for garnish

2 teaspoons shilgochu (Korean chile threads), for garnish

2 scallions, finely chopped, for garnish

FOR THE YANGNYUM SAUCE

2 tablespoons gochugaru

1 tablespoon soy sauce

1 scallion, minced

2 teaspoons minced garlic

1 Cut between the bones to create smaller pieces of meat with a bone attached to each. Soak the ribs in water to cover for about 1 hour to draw out the blood. Drain the ribs.

2 Put the ribs in a large pot with 1 teaspoon salt and 1 gallon (3.8 L) water, onion, scallions, garlic, and ginger. Bring the pot to a boil, then reduce the heat and let the pot cook at a simmer for 1 hour and 15 minutes. Add the radish and let cook for at least another half hour or until the meat and radishes are tender.

3 Leaving the ribs and radish in the pot, remove the rest of the vegetables and aromatics and discard them.

4 Turn off the heat and skim off any fat. (At this point you can cool the soup and refrigerate it to serve the next day. The fat will solidify, making it easier to remove.)

5 Stir in the soy sauce and fish sauce, if using. Add the noodles and let them simmer for about 5 to 7 minutes, or until they are cooked through. Add the pepper, and more salt to taste.

6 To make the yangnyum sauce, whisk all the ingredients together in a small mixing bowl.

7 Serve the soup garnished with egg ribbons, shilgochu, and scallions, and place small bowls of yangnyum sauce on the side.

SEE HOW-TO ON FOLLOWING PAGES

1 Cut the short ribs between the bones into individual ribs.

2 Soak the ribs in a large bowl covered with water for 1 hour.

3 You'll see the blood start to leach out of the ribs, which makes for a clearer soup. Drain the ribs and rinse them under cold running water.

4 Prepare all the other ingredients for the soup.

CONTINUES

7

5 Cut the radish into thin quarters.

6 Simmer the onion and aromatics for 1 hour 15 minutes, then add the radish and cook for another ½ hour, or until the meat and radishes are tender.

7 Leave the ribs and radish in the pot and pick out the rest of the vegetables and the aromatics with tongs and discard them.

8 Add the soy sauce and fish sauce.

9 Add the noodles and simmer until they are cooked through, then garnish the dish.

KALBI JJIM

BRAISED BEEF SHORT RIBS

This is a traditional special-occasion dish, and it is also great for the winter when cooking it keeps you warm by the stove. Koreans usually just boil the meat—after the bones are soaked and blanched to remove impurities—but I like to apply some French technique and braise it with just a little red wine for deeper flavor. Garnish this with ribbons of cooked egg, Korean chile threads, and sliced scallions, and of course serve it with plenty of rice.

Serves 4 to 6

5 pounds (2.3 kg) bone-in beef short ribs, cut between the bones to create smaller pieces of meat with a bone attached to each

1 large white onion, quartered

8 cloves garlic

⅓ cup (80 g) peeled and roughly chopped fresh ginger

¾ cup (180 ml) soy sauce

½ cup (110 g) packed brown sugar

½ cup (120 ml) mirin or 2 tablespoons honey

½ cup (120 ml) red wine

1 cup (240 g) chopped Baechu Kimchi (page 102), with juice

1 teaspoon freshly ground black pepper

2 cups (280 g) diced carrots

2 cups (260 g) diced moo or daikon radish

1 cup (105 g) roasted, peeled chestnuts

7 dried jujubes (see page 12)

1 tablespoon pine nuts, for garnish

Egg ribbons from 2 large eggs(see step 9, page 238), for garnish

1 tablespoon shilgochu (Korean chile threads), for garnish

⅓ cup (20 g) thinly sliced scallions, for garnish

1   Rinse the ribs and soak them in cold water to cover for 30 minutes to draw out the blood. Drain them and rinse again, then place in a pot with cold water to cover. Bring the pot to a boil, let cook for 2 to 3 minutes, then remove the short ribs and discard water. Rinse the ribs and clean the pot.

2   Put the onion, garlic, and ginger in a food processor or blender and process until it is a chunky puree.

3   Put the puree in a large pot with the ribs, soy sauce, brown sugar, mirin, red wine, kimchi, and black pepper. Add enough water to just cover the meat. Bring to a boil over medium-high heat, then cover the pot and lower the heat so that the pot cooks at a simmer for 1 hour.

4   Add the carrots, radish, chestnuts, and jujubes and let the pot simmer, uncovered, for another 30 minutes.

5   Serve the stew in deep bowls, garnished with pine nuts, egg ribbons, chile threads, and scallions. This is even better reheated the next day.

AL GYERAN JJIM
STEAMED EGGS WITH SALTED POLLACK ROE

Let's talk salted pollack roe: Yes, it's bright pink, seasoned with MSG, and blasted with food coloring, but it is beloved by Koreans. My grandmother used to eat it all the time, so serving it today fills me with so many good memories of her. You'll only need one lobe for this elegant and subtly flavored steamed egg dish, which is also served as *banchan*: You can eat the leftovers as my grandmother did, topped with slivers of red chile and scallion and seasoned with salt, black pepper, and sesame oil. Note that you don't want to use any scallion greens in the eggs, as they'll turn brown from the long cooking, but you can use the tops to garnish the dish, if you like. This is also traditionally made in a small (750 ml) *ttukbaegi* bowl, but you can substitute a clay or ceramic baking dish.

NOTE: Salted pollack roe lobes are sold frozen in a box. To use it, let the block slowly defrost overnight in the refrigerator, then gently split the sacs apart. (Consume any leftovers within a week.) If you can't find salted pollack roe or don't want to consume MSG or food coloring, you can use 2 ounces (57 g) fish eggs or caviar.

Serves 4

6 large eggs, beaten

1 teaspoon kosher salt

6 ounces (170 g) Master Anchovy stock (page 228)

1 lobe or sac seasoned pollack roe, at room temperature (see Note)

1 tablespoon minced scallion, white parts only, green parts reserved for garnish (optional)

1 Place the eggs, salt, and stock in a 3-cup (720 ml) ttukbaegi or heat-proof baking dish, then squeeze nearly all the roe from the roe sac into the dish. Set some roe aside to use as garnish, and discard the roe sac. Add the scallion whites and gently stir so that everything is mixed together. The scallion will float, and the roe will settle to the bottom.

2 Gently place the baking dish in a large stockpot, and fill the stockpot with water to come halfway up the sides of the baking dish.

3 Bring the water to a boil, then cover the pot and let the baking dish steam until the eggs are set, about 15 to 20 minutes.

4 Garnish with extra roe and the minced scallion tops if desired, and serve hot or at room temperature in the bowl or baking dish. This should be eaten the day it is made.

SEOLLONG TANG

BEEF BONE BROTH

This isn't difficult to make, but it does require the patience to cook the bones in several changes of boiling water, coaxing out ever more milky, flavorful goodness from the marrow in the bones each time. If you boil the bones at a medium boil, rather than a simmer, the broth will come out so much thicker and creamier—the results are beyond restorative.

FOR THE SOUP

5 pounds (2.3 kg) beef bones, preferably leg and knuckle bones

1 pound (455 g) brisket

2 scallions

6 whole garlic cloves

FOR THE GARNISH

Flaky sea salt

1 scallion, thinly sliced

Yangnyum Sauce (page 217)

1   Rinse the bones and then place them in a medium pot with water to cover for 30 minutes, then drain the bones, leaving them in the pot.

2   Cover bones again with clean water, and bring just to a medium boil over medium-high heat. Let cook until the liquid has reduced by half, about 30 to 45 minutes.

3   Strain the cooking liquid into a large, heatproof container and set it aside.

4   Add the brisket, scallions, and garlic to the pot with the bones and add ice-cold water to cover.

5   Bring the pot to a boil, then lower the heat to medium-high and leave at a medium boil for another 30 to 45 minutes. Then strain the liquid into the heatproof container: You should notice a deepening milkiness in the broth.

6   Repeat step 5 one or even two more times, if you have patience, each time pouring the liquid into the heatproof container. Discard the bones, scallions, and garlic cloves but set the brisket aside.

7   To serve the soup, bring the cooking liquid in the pot and everything in the heatproof container to a simmer in a stockpot. Slice the reserved brisket, and garnish hot bowls of the broth with a few brisket slices, a sprinkle of salt, and sliced scallions. Place small bowls of yangyeom sauce on the side.

MYEOLCHI GUKMUL

MASTER ANCHOVY STOCK

This is my master anchovy stock, the secret sauce I use both as a broth and to add flavor to other dishes in so many ways. It is a little more intense than Japanese stock, which is a close cousin. I usually save the seaweed from this recipe and toss it into the Kong Namul (page 90), or soybean sprout *banchan*, or add it to noodle soups.

Makes 4 cups (960 ml)

¼ cup (25 g/
  about 10) dried
  anchovies, heads
  and guts removed

¼ medium onion

5 cloves garlic

5 small dried
  shiitake mushrooms

4-inch (10 cm) piece
  dashima seaweed
  (kombu)

1   In a dry saucepan over medium-high heat, toast the anchovies just until they begin to smell fragrant. (You can skip this step if you want a lightly flavored stock.)

2   In a pot, combine the anchovies with the remaining ingredients and 5 cups (1.2 L) water.

3   Bring the water to a low simmer over medium heat and let cook for 30 minutes.

4   Strain out and discard the solids, reserving the dashima for another use, if desired. Store the stock in an airtight container in the refrigerator for 3 or 4 weeks.

Noodles, rice, and dumplings—or *myeon*, *hap*, and *mandu*, respectively—are the things that fill you up. With the exception of the plain, perfectly cooked rice on page 15, which is the foundation of the typical Korean meal, most of the recipes in this chapter were traditionally informal, snacky, quickly eaten foods meant to tide you over. (Though modern dining trends are changing that.) After work, you'd take leftover rice and throw together *kimchi bokkeum hap* (kimchi fried rice), or grab a few frozen mandu or dumplings from the freezer. Maybe you'd go out to lunch and grab a seaweed-rice roll called *kimhop*, or get a bowl of the springy black bean noodles called *jjeol myeon*, then go back to work.

Like soups and stews, our cravings for these dishes are often very specific: We want cold noodles to cool us down in summer, *japchae* for celebrations, mandu for holidays. And, of course, *juk* when we're sick. Koreans use many kinds of rice, grains, and noodles, and most of these dishes are traditionally built around one specific variety—these are shown in detail in the Korean Kitchen on page 10.

MYEON, BAP & MANDU

NOODLES, RICE & DUMPLINGS

BASIC UDON NOODLE SOUP

The Japanese annexed Korea back in the early twentieth century, and we were under Japanese rule for nearly thirty-five years. Today there is most definitely a Japanese influence on Korean food. Udon soup—a light, dried fish and seaweed broth filled with the thick, wheat-flour noodles called udon (see page 11)—is but one example. Today the simple style of udon soup here is often eaten as street food—you can nearly always get it with market fish cakes (see page 60) threaded on skewers. Street udon is tasty, for sure, but I always prefer to go without the flavor enhancers that are ubiquitous in mainstream Korean cooking these days. This is a very simple version of udon soup that you can dress up any way you like: with vegetables, dried seaweed, shredded meats, or a soft-cooked egg (see step 3 on page 245). This dish remains a kid favorite, as it still involves one of their favorite white foods: thick, glossy noodles, ideal for practicing over-the-top slurps!

NOTE: Fresh Korean udon noodles, which look like thick, glossy spaghetti, are made from wheat flour and found in 6- or 8-ounce (170 or 225 g) packages, sometimes in the freezer section. If they are frozen, do not defrost them before you use them. If you can't find them, try thicker Japanese udon, or any fresh wheat flour pasta, though the Asian versions have more chewy bounce than Italian noodles.

Serves 4

6 large dried anchovies, heads and guts removed

3 cloves garlic

4-inch (10 cm) piece dried kelp

6 cups (1.4 L) cold water

1 teaspoon fish sauce, plus more to taste

1 tablespoon soy sauce, plus more to taste

12 to 16 ounces (340 to 455 g) Korean udon noodles (see Note)

1 scallion, thinly sliced

1   Tie the anchovies, garlic, and kelp in a piece of cheesecloth and place in a stockpot with the water.

2   Bring to a simmer over medium heat and let cook for 15 to 20 minutes.

3   Reduce the heat to medium-low, so the broth stays hot, and remove and discard the cheesecloth. Stir in the fish sauce and soy sauce, adding more as desired.

4   Meanwhile, bring a separate pot of water to a boil over high heat, then cook and drain the noodles according to the package directions.

5   Serve the noodles in bowls covered with the hot broth, garnished with the scallion.

JJAJANG MYEON

BLACK BEAN NOODLES

Jjajang myeon—fresh wheat noodles in a sweet-savory black bean sauce with garlic and ginger—can be had in South Korea anywhere, anytime, even delivered to you on the edge of the Han River in Seoul. (Some specialty restaurants focus just on this dish and make the noodles from scratch—if you're lucky you might get a glimpse of the noodle-maker hand-pulling the noodles.) Both the wheat noodles and the black bean sauce are Chinese in origin; this also goes really well with the Kkanpoong Shrimp (page 166). You want lots of this sauce on your noodles, so pile it on, and don't forget to wear a bib if you're wearing nice clothes!

NOTE: Traditionally this dish is made with fresh Chinese-style "hand-pulled" noodles. If you live near a Chinatown, you may be able to find a noodle-maker; if not, use fresh udon noodles as described in the note on page 233.

Serves 4 to 6

1 pound (455 g) pork belly or pork jowl, cut into ½-inch (12 mm) cubes

1 teaspoon kosher salt

½ teaspoon freshly ground black pepper

1 tablespoon mirin

1 tablespoon minced garlic

1 tablespoon minced peeled fresh ginger

¼ cup (60 ml) olive oil

1 pound (455 g) white onions, finely diced

¾ cup (180 ml) Korean black bean paste

1 tablespoon packed brown sugar

3 tablespoons rice wine vinegar

3 cups (720 ml) Master Anchovy Stock (page 228)

½ pound (225 g) Korean green squash (see Note, page 39) or zucchini, finely diced

1 pound (455 g) large Yukon gold potatoes, finely diced

1 tablespoon potato starch stirred into 3 tablespoons cold water

1 pound (455 g) Korean udon noodles, (see Note, page 233)

3 Kirby or small Persian cucumbers, julienned

Danmuji (sweet pickled radish; see Note, page 175), for serving

Baechu Kimchi (page 102), for serving

1   In a mixing bowl, combine the pork cubes with the salt, pepper, mirin, garlic, and ginger and use your clean hands to massage the seasonings into the pork. Set aside for 30 minutes to 1 hour.

2   In a large saucepan, heat the oil over medium heat. Cook the onions, stirring occasionally, until they are soft, about 7 to 8 minutes.

3   Add the seasoned pork to the pan and let it cook, stirring occasionally, until it is almost cooked through, about 10 to 12 minutes.

4   Stir in the black bean paste, brown sugar, and vinegar and let everything cook, stirring occasionally, for 5 minutes.

CONTINUES

5   Increase the heat to medium-high and
    add the anchovy stock, squash, and
    potatoes. Bring to a boil, then reduce
    the heat so that the sauce cooks at a
    simmer for about 30 minutes.

6   Stir in the potato starch slurry, then
    increase the heat so that the sauce
    cooks at a low boil just until the sauce
    begins to thicken. Turn off the heat
    and keep the sauce warm.

7   In a separate large pot of boiling water,
    cook the udon noodles according to
    the package instructions, then drain
    and divide the noodles among 4 to 6
    bowls. Top each bowl with a healthy
    portion of the sauce and a small pile of
    julienned cucumbers.

8   Serve immediately, letting each
    person mix the noodles and sauce as
    they like, adding pickled radish and
    kimchi to their taste.

JAPCHAE

STIR-FRIED SWEET POTATO NOODLES

This vegetable-heavy noodle stir-fry is a traditional *janchi*, or party dish for Korean celebrations and family gatherings. I like to make it for a big group of people because it does require a bit of time to make. You have to prepare each of the vegetables separately, so each is perfectly cooked, and as a result, the flavors are delicious and pure. Slinky sweet potato noodles—called *dang myeon*, shown on page 11—are especially springy and fun to eat, and leftovers can be easily warmed up in a frying pan: The fat and cloudy cold noodles return to their glossy luster when they're kissed by the heat.

Secret trick: Double the vegetables when you prep this dish, and you'll have extra for Bibimbop (page 246).

Serves 4 to 6

FOR THE NOODLES

6 ounces (170 g) dried dang myeon

1 tablespoon sesame oil

2 teaspoons soy sauce

1 teaspoon granulated sugar

FOR THE VEGETABLES

Grapeseed or olive oil, for pan-frying

½ white onion, thinly sliced

Kosher salt

1 medium carrot, cut into matchstick-size pieces or julienned

½ pound (225 g) cremini mushrooms, stemmed and thinly sliced

1 thumb-sized knob peeled fresh ginger, grated

1 bunch spinach, arugula, green cabbage, or Swiss chard leaves, thinly sliced (optional)

1 small red, yellow, or orange bell pepper, cut into matchstick-size pieces or thinly sliced

1 tablespoon finely grated garlic

1 tablespoon soy sauce

1 tablespoon granulated sugar

1 teaspoon freshly ground black pepper

2 teaspoons sesame oil

1 tablespoon toasted sesame seeds

FOR SERVING

1 tablespoon grapeseed or olive oil

3 raw egg yolks, beaten

1 tablespoon toasted sesame seeds

2 scallions, thinly sliced on the bias

CONTINUES

1   Prepare the noodles: Bring a large pot of water to a boil and cook the noodles according to the package directions until they are cooked through, about 5 to 7 minutes. Drain the noodles and rinse them under cold running water until the noodles feel cool to the touch.

2   Shake off any excess water from the noodles and place them in a large mixing bowl with the sesame oil, soy sauce, and sugar. Toss until the noodles are well coated, then set the bowl aside.

3   Prepare the vegetables: In a skillet, heat a tablespoon of oil over medium to medium-high heat. Cook the onion until soft, stirring occasionally, about 3 to 5 minutes. Season with a pinch of salt and add them to the bowl with the noodles.

4   Add the carrot to the skillet and cook, stirring once or twice, just until it begins to soften, about a minute and a half. Add them to the bowl with the noodles.

5   Add another tablespoon of oil to the skillet, then cook the mushrooms with the grated ginger, stirring occasionally, until the mushrooms release all their liquid and the pan is almost dry. Add them to the bowl with the noodles.

6   If using the greens, add another tablespoon of oil to the skillet, and cook the greens, stirring occasionally, until they just soften, about 2 minutes. Drain off any liquid from the pan and place the wilted greens in a colander set into a bowl or the sink to drain.

7   Add another tablespoon of oil to the skillet, and cook the bell pepper, stirring occasionally, until they just soften, about 2 minutes. Add them to the bowl with the noodles.

8   Squeeze excess water from the greens with your hands and place them in the bowl with the noodles. Toss the vegetables and the noodles together with the garlic, soy sauce, sugar, black pepper, sesame oil, and sesame seeds. Taste for seasoning, adding more soy sauce, sugar, etc. as desired. Set the noodles aside while you make the eggs.

9   To serve: In a nonstick skillet, heat the oil over low heat. Pour in the egg yolks so that they cover the bottom of the pan in a thin layer, and let them cook until they are set. Remove the omelet to a cutting board, roll, and slice into thin ribbons.

10 Top the noodles and vegetables with the egg ribbons, sesame seeds, and sliced scallions, and serve immediately.

JJEOL MYEON

COLD SPICY NOODLES WITH VEGETABLES AND SOFT-BOILED EGGS

Koreans appreciate texture as much as flavor in their food, and what makes this cold dish special is the chewy bite of the *jjeol myeon* noodles shown on page 11, which are made of wheat flour, cornstarch, and cooking wine. (Jjeol myeon basically means "chewy noodle.") For Koreans, jjeol myeon is a quick, refreshing dinner on a hot summer's day: The noodles are cooked just to tender, then tossed with a spicy sauce and raw vegetables for crunch and contrast. Technically, this is a *bibim*-style cold noodle dish: *Bibim* means "mixed up," as in tossing everything together in a bowl for a one-dish meal. Once you master this recipe, I recommend you do as Koreans do: Take any cooked noodle you like, then mix it up—bibim!—with the spicy sauce in this recipe and whatever thinly sliced raw or pickled vegetables you have on hand.

NOTE: If you can't find jjeol myeon noodles, a good substitute is a chewy noodle like ramen, either fresh or instant.

The gochujang-based sauce here is a base Korean cooks adapt to use in a lot of things, the way Italians would turn to a marinara. With a few adjustments it can go on the squid stir-fry on page 64, work as a glaze for barbecue, or even serve as a quick sauce for bibimbop (page 246). Here rice wine vinegar and lemon juice are added, which brightens up what is meant to be a refreshing dish.

Serves 4

FOR THE SAUCE

- ¼ cup (60 ml) gochujang
- 3 tablespoons packed brown sugar
- 2 tablespoons gochugaru
- 2 tablespoons soy sauce
- 2 tablespoons minced garlic
- 2 tablespoons toasted sesame seeds
- 3 tablespoons sesame oil
- 1 tablespoon rice wine vinegar
- 2 teaspoons lemon juice

FOR THE NOODLES

- 1 pound (455 g) jjol myeon noodles
- 1 cup (115 g) raw zucchini or cucumbers, cut into strips as per page 14
- 1 cup (30 g) perilla or shiso leaves, cut into thick ribbons
- 1 cup (55 g) thinly sliced scallions
- 1 cup (90 g) mung bean or soybean sprouts (optional)
- 4 soft-boiled eggs (page 245, step 3), halved
- 1 tablespoon toasted black or white sesame seeds

1 Make the sauce: In a small mixing bowl, combine all the ingredients for the sauce until well incorporated, then set aside.

2 Make the noodles: In a large pot of boiling water, cook the noodles until just al dente, about 3 to 4 minutes. Immediately drain them and rinse under running water until all the noodles feel cool to the touch. (This keeps them from overcooking, but also washes away residual starches, keeping them firm and chewy.) Let them drain for 5 minutes.

3 Place the drained noodles in a large serving or salad bowl. Add the reserved sauce and toss the noodles until they are well coated.

4 Add the zucchini, perilla leaves, scallions, mung beans, if using, eggs, and sesame seeds, and toss until well mixed.

5 Serve immediately.

BIBIM NAENG MYEON

SPICY CHEWY NOODLES WITH CHILLED BEEF BROTH

This cold noodle dish is meant for summer, and it is so uniquely good it will almost make you look forward to sticky, hot weather. The broth—a mix of stock and a little fermented radish brine and mustard powder—is frozen until it becomes a savory, tart slushie, which is then served in deep bowls with chewy buckwheat noodles called *naeng myeon* (basically "cold noodle") and a spicy-sweet sauce. This you mix up—*bibim*—with fresh and preserved vegetables and top with perfectly boiled eggs. Though the broth is tamed slightly by the chill, it should still pack a punch: It's hot thanks to the chile and the hot mustard powder and a little funky thanks to the brine from *dongchimi*, or whole Korean moo radishes fermented in water with ginger and sweet Asian pear. (Nobody really sells dongchimi—it's an old-fashioned thing—so you have to make it yourself.) Note that you can follow your own recipe for hard-boiling eggs, but I prefer mine more soft-boiled, as they just taste that much better.

NOTE: Often you can only find naeng myeon noodles, shown on page 11, with a packet of processed sauce to make this dish. I just toss the pre-made sauce and use the noodles. For the beef broth, use your favorite or follow the instructions for the broth in Sogogi Moo Guk on page 192.

Serves 4

FOR THE BROTH

1 cup (240 ml) Master Anchovy Stock (page 228)

2 cups (480 ml) Beef Broth (see Note)

1 teaspoon granulated sugar

½ to 1 cup (60 to 120 ml) Dongchimi juice (page 119)

1 teaspoon rice wine vinegar

½ teaspoon kosher salt

½ teaspoon Colman's mustard powder, or to taste

FOR THE SAUCE

¾ cup (75 g) grated, peeled Asian pear

1 teaspoon minced peeled fresh ginger

½ teaspoon minced garlic

¼ cup (60 ml) brown rice syrup

¼ cup (60 ml) gochugaru

1 tablespoon gochujang

1 tablespoon toasted sesame seeds

2 teaspoons kosher salt

1 teaspoon soy sauce

FOR SERVING

2 large eggs

1 pound (455 g) *naeng myeon* noodles (see Note)

1 cup (115 g) julienned Asian cucumber, watery seeds removed

1 cup (115 g) Nabak Kimchi (page 114) or Moo Malleng e Muchim (page 88)

2 scallions, thinly sliced

1 tablespoon toasted sesame seeds

CONTINUES

You can make a plain,
non-spicy naeng myeon,
shown left, by omitting
the sauce. Just double
the slushy broth and
serve it with extra
mustard on the side.

1   Prepare the broth: In a shallow, flat-bottomed, freezer-safe container, combine the ingredients for the broth. Place in the freezer until the broth has the consistency of a slushie or a frozen drink, about 45 minutes to 1 hour. (If it over-freezes, take it out and let it sit until it's soft enough to crush with a fork.)

2   Make the sauce: In a small bowl, combine the ingredients for the sauce and set aside.

3   Prepare the dish: Bring a small pot of water to boil. Gently drop in the eggs and boil for 7 minutes. Remove the eggs from the pot and cover with cold water, cracking them gently against the side of the pot so that their shells break slightly. Empty the pot and set it aside.

4   Bring a large pot of water to a boil and cook the noodles for 3 minutes.

5   Immediately drain the noodles and rinse them under running water until all the noodles feel cool to the touch. (This keeps them from overcooking, but also washes away residual starches, keeping them firm and chewy.) Set the noodles aside.

6   In a large mixing bowl, break it apart the frozen broth with a fork until it is soft and spoonable but still frozen.

7   Add the noodles and the sauce to the bowl and toss to mix.

8   Place a quarter of the noodles, sauce, and broth in each serving bowl.

9   Top each bowl with little piles of a quarter of the cucumber, a quarter of the pickled radish, a quarter of the scallions, a quarter of the sesame seeds, and then half an egg.

10 Serve immediately, letting each person mix and toss the noodles and toppings to their liking.

BIBIMBOP

This is one of my favorite breakfasts. It might be a challenge for some to have a rice bowl first thing in the morning, but we Asians do it all the time! This dish is great at every meal, though. If you think of the five vegetables listed below—chopped kale, shredded carrot, blanched green beans, and sautéed onions and mushrooms—as suggestions, they'll feel like a lot less work. You should use anything you want or have on hand; the key is just to cook or prep each one separately, so they retain their own texture and color. Koreans like spinach, carrots, cooked soybean sprouts, mushrooms, and wild ferns, but I tend to go for seasonality. In fact, traditionally you would just mix up last night's leftover vegetables or *banchan* with cooked rice and a spoonful of gochujang sauce, and that's the original bibimbop. The fried eggs are just an extra bonus—feel free to skip them, or even to augment them with a little bacon, Bulgogi (page 185), or any leftover BBQ meats.

NOTE: To sauté the onions and mushrooms, cook them in 2 tablespoons oil in a skillet over medium heat until they are soft.

Serves 6

FOR THE SAUCE

¼ cup (60 ml) gochujang

2 tablespoons packed dark brown sugar

2 tablespoons olive oil

1 tablespoon sesame oil

2 tablespoons rice wine vinegar

1 to 2 teaspoons gochugaru

FOR THE BIBIMBOP

6 cups (600 g) steamed short-grain (sushi) rice, kept warm

1 bunch kale or Swiss chard, leaves chopped into 1-inch (2.5 cm) pieces and, sautéed

2 large carrots, shredded or cut into 2 by ¼-inch (5 cm by 6 mm) matchstick strips

½ pound (225 g) green beans, blanched and cut into 1-inch (2.5 cm) pieces

2 medium white onions, thinly sliced and sautéed (see Note)

½ pound (225 g) fresh cremini or button mushrooms, thinly sliced and sautéed (see Note)

6 large eggs, fried sunny-side up

Sliced scallions, for garnish

Toasted sesame seeds, for garnish

1   Make the sauce: In a small bowl or jar, combine the gochujang, brown sugar, olive oil, sesame oil, vinegar, and gochugaru, adjusting the vinegar and gochugaru to taste. Set aside.

2   Make the bibimbop: In each of 6 bowls, place a mound of rice and top it with the 5 to 7 different vegetables. Dollop the sauce around the bowl and top with an egg and some scallions and sesame seeds. Serve with extra sauce and encourage each diner to mix up their own bowl.

KIMBOP

These sushi-like Korean rolls—steamed seasoned rice and other ingredients tightly wrapped in sheets of roasted seaweed (see page 13) and sliced into rounds—were probably introduced to Korea during the Japanese occupation of the early twentieth century. They're larger than Japanese sushi, have more of that delicious seasoned rice, and are traditionally served without soy sauce or wasabi. For Koreans, kimbop is the quintessential picnic food, or something to eat on the go. (For kids, it's even a must-have in a lunch box.) We make these with almost any filling you can think of, and you don't have to stop at the ones I recommend below. Try adding thin slices of cucumber, any kind of kimchi, cooked bulgogi, the spicy squid on page 78, the Spam on page 188, or even canned tuna fish. If you do plan to make kimbop, invest in a sushi mat—a bamboo mat made for rice rolling. You can roll these without one, but it really eases the process.

NOTE: You can make the yellow pickled radish used in kimbop—*danmuji*—using the instructions on page 175, or just buy it in refrigerated plastic bags in most Korean supermarkets, usually next to the kimchi.

Makes 5 rolls

1 teaspoon grapeseed or olive oil

4 large eggs, beaten

1 bunch spinach or watercress

Kosher salt

1 carrot, cut into ½-inch (12 mm) wide strips

4 cups (368 g) cooked sushi or short-grain rice, still hot

2 tablespoons rice wine vinegar

5 sheets roasted seaweed

½ pound (225 g) yellow pickled radish (see Note), cut into long sticks

½ pound (225 g) crab stick (imitation crab), halved lengthwise

Sesame oil, for brushing

1   In a nonstick skillet over low heat, heat the oil. Pour in the eggs so that they cover the bottom of the pan in a thin layer, and let them cook until they are set. Remove the omelet to a cutting board and let it cool to room temperature before cutting it into thick ribbons as shown in the how-to on page 15.

2   Bring a large pot of salted water to a boil and prepare a mixing bowl with salted ice-cold water. Drop the spinach or watercress into the boiling water and let it cook just until it is wilted and turns bright green, about 7 seconds. Remove the greens from the water with tongs and place them in the ice water. Swish the greens around in the water with your hands until the greens have cooled, then drain them in a colander, squeezing out all the water with your hands.

3   In a skillet, heat 1 tablespoon water and a pinch of salt over medium heat and cook the carrot just until it begins to soften, about 2 minutes. Remove the carrot from the heat and set aside to cool.

4   When you're ready to form the kimbop, put the warm rice in a mixing bowl and mix in the vinegar and 1 teaspoon salt. Let cool slightly before forming the rolls.

5   Form the rolls according to the directions on pages 250–253. Slice the rolls into thick rounds and eat them the day they are made.

1 Season the rice when it has cooled to warm. Taste it, and add more vinegar or salt as needed.

2 Set the roasted seaweed on a bamboo mat, then place about $\frac{1}{2}$ cup (92 g) rice on the bottom half of the sheet.

3 Set up a small bowl of water and use wet fingers to spread the rice into a thin layer on the bottom two-thirds of the seaweed, dipping your fingers in the water as needed so that the rice doesn't stick to your hands. You want the rice to cover the roasted seaweed in an even layer.

4 Lay the cooked greens on the rice in a single layer near the bottom of the roasted seaweed, then place the yellow pickled radish, the carrots, a strip of egg, and the crab stick.

CONTINUES

5 Pick up the edge of the bamboo closest to you and fold it over the fillings.

6 Use your fingertips to tuck the kimbop up under the rolled edge of the bamboo, ensuring the wrapping is tight.

7 Hold the leading edge of the bamboo mat out and gently roll the bamboo over the kimbop, using your hands to pinch the kimbop into shape. If the seaweed doesn't stick together, use a few kernels of warm rice as glue.

8 Make sure the kimbop is tightly rolled by shaping it with the bamboo mat.

9 Release the kimbop by gently rolling it off the mat.

10 The kimbop should be perfectly sealed into shape. Prepare a small bowl with sesame oil. Coat your clean hands with the oil and gently rub the outside of the roasted seaweed. This prevents your roll from puckering and losing its shape, and it also adds flavor.

AL BOP

RICE WITH CAVIAR

This is one of many rice bowl dishes you'll find in Korea, often at restaurants that serve seafood. It's a treat to serve at home: The briny crunch of the caviar on top of the warm rice is a big draw— even my ten-year-old who is too picky for chicken pot pie will eat it. Serve this with soy sauce, rice wine vinegar, and sesame oil at the table so each person can adjust to their taste.

Serves 2

3 tablespoons
   salmon roe

1 cup (240 ml) soju
   or sake (optional)

4 cups (512 g)
   freshly cooked
   short-grain rice

2 tablespoons flying
   fish roe

3 tablespoons Butchu
   (Garlic Chive)
   Kimchi (page 116),
   thinly sliced

3 tablespoons thinly
   sliced scallions

1 tablespoon toasted
   sesame seeds

Soy sauce,
   for serving

Rice wine,
   for serving

Sesame oil,
   for serving

1   Put the salmon roe in a small mixing bowl and cover them with the soju, if using. (Skip this step if not.) Let it sit in the refrigerator for 1 hour, then drain off the liquor.

2   Place the hot rice in a large bowl and spoon both types of roe on top in little piles. Top the bowl with the chive kimchi, scallions, and sesame seeds.

3   Serve immediately with soy sauce, rice wine vinegar, and sesame oil on the side.

JUK

CONGEE

I ate so much *juk* when I was growing up, it took a long time for me to embrace having this regularly for dinner. But there's no denying it: This dish, essentially a savory rice porridge, is so very, very comforting—it's a must-make for me when a family member is under the weather or has a delicate stomach. If you don't have any stock on hand, you can also easily make it with water, and it'll still be wonderful. I often top it with a *gyeran jorim* (soy-marinated egg) or poached or fried egg, but you can eat it as is, or even top it with any protein you like.

Serves 2 to 4

2 cups (410 g) short-grain (sushi) rice

5 to 6 cups (1.2 to 1.4 L) Master Anchovy Stock

¼ teaspoon kosher salt

⅛ teaspoon freshly ground black pepper

2 thick slices fresh ginger

1 teaspoon soy sauce, plus more to taste

1 tablespoon thinly sliced scallions

2 to 4 Soy-Marinated Seven-Minute Eggs (page 30), poached eggs, or soft-boiled eggs (page 245, step 3; optional)

1 In a large saucepan, bring the rice and 5 cups (1.2 L) of the stock to a boil with the salt, black pepper, ginger, and soy sauce. Cover the pot and reduce the heat so that the congee cooks at a simmer for 35 minutes, stirring occasionally.

2 Uncover the pot, remove and discard the ginger slices, and add 1 more cup (240 ml) of the stock. Let cook for another 10 minutes, or until it is thick and the rice is soft and tender.

3 Serve the congee in bowls sprinkled with a little soy sauce and the scallions, topping each bowl with an egg, if desired.

KiMCHi FRiED RiCE

This is best made with day-old rice. I usually also make it with the oldest, stinkiest kimchi sitting in the back of my fridge, bringing it all back to deliciousness by sautéing it with a little sugar and rice wine vinegar, and sometimes the homemade Spam on page 188. Yes, you can use canned Spam, or bacon, if you like.

Serves 4

Grapeseed or olive oil

1 cup (115 g) cubed Spam

1 tablespoon unsalted butter

1¾ cups (490 g) Baechu Kimchi (page 102), cut into bite-size pieces

2 tablespoons rice wine vinegar

2 teaspoons granulated sugar

4 cups (820 g) cooked short-grain rice

Kosher salt

4 large eggs

Thinly sliced scallions (optional)

1   In a large skillet, heat 2 teaspoons oil over medium-high heat. Add the Spam and cook it, stirring occasionally, until it is brown on all sides, about 3 minutes. Remove from the pan and set aside.

2   Add the butter, kimchi, vinegar, and sugar, and cook, stirring occasionally, until the kimchi is heated through and softens slightly, about 3 minutes. Fold in the cooked rice and the Spam, taste for salt, and keep it warm while you cook the eggs.

3   In a medium skillet, heat 1 tablespoon oil over medium heat, and fry the eggs sunny-side up.

4   Top each plate of kimchi rice with one egg and garnish with sliced scallions, if using.

BASIC JAP GOK BOP

HEALTHY RICE

In Korea rice is the staple. Traditionally everyone gets their own bowl of rice, and they put a few bites of *banchan* or meat or fish on top of it. (The size of that bowl has decreased over the years, with carb-conscious eating.) Many Koreans, especially older ones, would tell you they don't feel like they've really eaten until they have rice. And when I was growing up, pearly white rice still signified wealth: If you had white rice, you were a fat cat. In the country, they ate a mix of grains and beans and white and brown rice called *jap gok bop* because it was cheaper. Now we all prefer the multi-grain, because we know a lot more about health and nutrition; we call this "healthy rice" mix. This version is simpler than most jap gok bop, because it is missing beans, but you can add them or any grain shown on page 13. The key is to soak everything in advance, and not to add salt, because the rest of the meal provides that.

Makes 5 cups (920 g)

1 cup (195 g) short-grain brown rice

2 cups (400 g) short-grain white rice

½ cup (200 g) millet

1   In a medium saucepan, combine the rices, and millet with 1 quart (960 ml) water and let them soak for 1 hour.

2   Bring to a boil, cover, and then reduce the heat to a low simmer. Cook until the grains are tender, about 25 minutes. Serve hot in individual bowls.

TTEOKBOKKI

SAUTÉED RICE CAKES

Tteokbokki is quintessential Korean street food, as well known as it is easy to make. Thick, chewy *tteok*, or rice cakes (see page 10), are simmered in a sweet-spicy gochujang sauce, their ample starches melting into the pot, making the dish thick and silky. When I was growing up in Korea in the 1970s, cheap and fast little tteokbokki places were just starting to pop up, thanks to one lady in particular who ran a popular stand in the neighborhood of Shin Dang Dong in Seoul. Eventually the area became *the* place to get tteokbokki from dozens of vendors who each prepared theirs with slightly different variations. To that end, I wanted to give you two recipes for this dish: Version 1 is the super-fast, bright-red, one-pot version most people make at home. Version 2 starts with toasted gochujang and umami-rich doenjang, which gives the dish a more complex, slow-cooked flavor, and also has vegetables and toasted rice cakes— my totally non-traditional addition, because I love that crunchy texture. Version 2 was developed by my sous chef at Insa, Yong Shin, at his insistence that the sauce be more flavorful. It's a company-worthy version of tteokbokki, especially with a soft-boiled egg. But rest assured, both are delicious.

NOTE : Rice cakes last about 2 weeks in the fridge and 6 weeks in the freezer. If they are frozen, soak them in a bowl of cold water until they have defrosted. These days you can find brown rice cakes, and you can use those, too, if you want.

Rice cakes are all about texture. Either you love them, or you don't get them at all. With mass production, rice cakes are now everyday food, but they started out as something for special occasions. You eat them for New Year's Day in the soup on page 194, on your birthday, and when babies turn one hundred days old, an important milestone in Korean culture. FYI, you'll see rice cakes spelled as either *dduk* or *tteok*, both of which are pronounced the same way, like "tduck." Koreans use a "td" sound, best represented in English by the double d or double t, though neither is a perfect match.

TTEOKBOKKI 1   Serves 4

½ cup (120 ml) gochujang

2 tablespoons honey

1 tablespoon gochugaru

2 tablespoons rice wine

1 tablespoon soy sauce

1 pound (450 g) frozen or fresh rice cakes (see Note)

1 bunch scallions, halved lengthwise and thinly sliced (see page 14), white and green parts separated

1 tablespoon toasted sesame seeds

1   In a medium saucepan, combine the gochujang, honey, gochugaru, rice wine, and soy sauce with 1 cup (240ml) water and bring to a simmer over medium heat.

2   Add the rice cakes and let them cook, stirring often, until the sauce begins to thicken and coat the rice cakes, about 3 minutes.

3   Add just the whites of the scallions, and let them cook for 3 to 5 minutes, or until they begin to soften. Stir in the rest of the scallions and the sesame seeds and turn off the heat. Serve immediately.

TTEOKBOKKI 2 Serves 4 to 6

FOR THE SAUCE

2 tablespoons vegetable oil

½ cup (120 ml) gochujang

3 tablespoons doenjang

2 teaspoons soy sauce

3 teaspoons honey

1 tablespoon gochugaru

½ cup (120 ml) Master Anchovy Stock (page 228)

1 tablespoon rice wine vinegar

FOR THE NOODLES AND VEGETABLES

3 tablespoons vegetable oil

1 pound (450 g) rice cakes, fresh or defrosted (see Note, page 262)

½ pound (225 g) fresh or defrosted market fish cakes, cut into ¼-inch (6 mm) slices (see page 60)

1 cup (100 g) julienned white or yellow onions

1 cup (120 g) julienned carrot

1 cup (110 g) thinly sliced scallions

2 cups (140 g) napa cabbage, cut into ½-inch (12 mm) ribbons

Kosher salt

Freshly ground black pepper

4 to 6 soft-boiled eggs (page 245, step 3; optional)

1 Make the sauce: In a large saucepan, heat the oil over medium heat. Add the gochujang and doenjang and let them toast in the hot oil for 5 minutes or until they begin to brown, using a spatula to stir them almost constantly. Be careful not to let them burn.

2 Whisk in the soy sauce, honey, gochugaru, stock, and vinegar until they are well combined. Increase the heat to medium-high and let the mixture simmer, stirring often, for about 7 minutes, or until the sauce is thick enough to coat the back of a spoon. Scrape the bottom of the pot frequently so the sauce does not scorch.

3 Strain the sauce through a chinois or fine-mesh sieve and set aside. (This can be made up to 2 weeks in advance and kept refrigerated.)

4 Make the noodles and vegetables: Heat 1 tablespoon of the oil in a large cast-iron skillet or frying pan (not nonstick) over medium heat. Place the rice cakes in a single layer in the skillet (you might have to do this in batches) and cook, turning them occasionally, until they are browned on both sides, about 2 minutes. Remove from the skillet and set aside.

5 In the same pan, add another tablespoon of the oil. Working over medium heat, cook the fish cakes, stirring them often for a few minutes, or until they are heated through. Remove them from the skillet and set them aside with the rice cakes.

6 Add the remaining tablespoon oil to the skillet and, working over medium-high heat, cook the onion, carrot, scallions, and cabbage, stirring often, until the vegetables have softened and slightly charred. Season to taste with salt and pepper.

7 Lower the heat to medium and return the fish cakes and rice cakes to the pan. Drizzle the sauce into the pan, tossing until everything is well coated and the sauce is heated through.

8 Serve immediately, topped with a soft-boiled egg, if desired.

GOGI MANDU

MEAT DUMPLINGS

The dumplings I make at the Good Fork are semi-famous, having won on *Throwdown with Bobby Flay*. Those are a hybrid of Japanese *gyoza* (with a very thin wrapper), Chinese dumplings (I use hoisin and dark soy sauce), and the Korean *mandu* or *mandoo* I grew up with, which come with chive and a bit of tofu, making the meatball inside silky and, well, less like a heavy meatball. These have a bit of sweetness from the honey or brown rice syrup, a little tang from kimchi juice or vinegar, and a little crunch from the sprouts—a real Korean mandu at heart.

NOTE: To cook frozen dumplings, follow the same procedure for fresh dumplings, but with ⅛ inch (8 mm) water so they steam a little longer and cook through.

Making 100 dumplings at a time sounds daunting, but it is the only way to do it. Gather a few friends, make the dumplings together, then tuck them—packaged by the dozen—into the freezer for weeks to come.

Makes about 100 dumplings

4 cups (360 g) mung bean sprouts

Canola oil

2 large onions, finely diced

½ cup (70 g) minced garlic

½ cup (50 g) minced peeled fresh ginger

1 pound (455 g) garlic chives, thinly sliced

12 ounces (340 g) firm tofu, crumbled

2 tablespoons honey or brown rice syrup

⅓ cup (75 ml) soy sauce

2 tablespoons Baechu Kimchi juice (page 102) or rice wine vinegar

1 tablespoon kosher salt, plus more to taste

1 tablespoon freshly ground black pepper

1 pound (455 g) ground beef

1 pound (455 g) ground pork

2 packages (16 ounces/ 455 g each) Shanghai-style dumpling wrappers

Dumpling Dipping Sauce, recipe follows

1. Bring a medium saucepan of water to a boil. Cook the sprouts in the boiling water for 4 minutes, then immediately remove them to a colander in the sink and rinse them with cold running water until all the sprouts are cool. Squeeze as much of the water from the sprouts as you can with clean hands and then finely chop them. Let them continue to drain in the colander while you prepare the rest of the filling.

2. In a skillet, heat 2 teaspoons oil over medium heat and sauté the onions, garlic, and ginger until the onions are translucent and slightly caramelized. Add the chives and cook just to soften them, about 1 minute more. Transfer the mixture to a large bowl and let cool.

3. Once the onions have cooled, add the tofu, honey, soy sauce, kimchi juice, salt, and pepper and mix well. Add the meat and chopped sprouts to the bowl and mix it with the seasonings until you can see that the sprouts, chives, and tofu are evenly distributed throughout the meat.

4. In a small skillet, heat a thin layer of oil over medium heat. Cook a small spoonful of the meat mixture, then taste and adjust the seasoning of the meat with more salt, if necessary.

CONTINUES

5   Prepare a small dish of water and line several baking sheets with parchment paper. Place about 1 tablespoon filling in each dumpling wrapper. Using your finger, paint a little water around the edge of the wrapper. Fold the wrapper in half and pinch the edges closed, or make it fancier by forming a few pleats. Place each finished dumpling on the baking sheet, repeating until you've used all the filling. Freeze the dumplings directly on the baking sheet until they harden, then pack them into plastic freezer bags, where they will last 3 to 4 months. (They do not refrigerate well.)

6   To cook fresh or frozen dumplings, heat a nonstick frying pan or well-seasoned cast-iron skillet with just enough canola oil to coat the bottom. Add just enough dumplings so that they are not overcrowded and don't touch. Brown the dumplings on their bottoms—this takes about a minute for fresh and slightly longer for frozen—then add about ¼ inch (6 mm) water, cover the skillet, and steam the dumplings until nearly all the water evaporates.

7   Remove the cover and let the dumplings fry again, just long enough to crisp them slightly, then serve them immediately with the dipping sauce.

DUMPLING DIPPING SAUCE
Makes about ¾ cup (180 ml)

½ cup (120 ml) soy sauce

½ cup (120 ml) rice wine vinegar

¼ cup (55 g) packed brown sugar

1 tablespoon sesame seeds

½ teaspoon gochugaru

1   In a small saucepan, bring the soy sauce, vinegar, and brown sugar to a simmer over medium-high heat, stirring so that the sugar dissolves. Once it does, remove from the heat and let the mixture cool. Feel free to add less sugar if you like.

2   Add the sesame seeds and gochugaru before serving. This sauce keeps well in the refrigerator indefinitely and can also be multiplied, though you'll want to start with slightly less vinegar and adjust to taste.

YACHAE MANDU

VEGETABLE DUMPLINGS

Like Japchae (page 237), vegetable dumplings illustrate how to cook vegetables properly: Cooking each one separately is really important. Vegetables can contain a lot of water, and for successful dumplings, you will want to cook some of the moisture out without overcooking them, and the only way to make that happen is to prep them one at a time. To that end, think of this recipe as a guide to making up your own fillings with whatever is on hand, in season, or about to go bad in your fridge.

NOTE: To cook frozen dumplings, follow the same procedure for fresh dumplings, but with ⅓ inch (8 mm) water so they steam a little longer and cook through.

Makes about 100 dumplings

Grapeseed or olive oil, for pan-frying

1 large white onion, minced

¼ cup (35 g) minced garlic

⅓ cup (45 g) minced peeled fresh ginger

1 pound (455 g) shiitake or cremini mushrooms, sliced

Kosher salt

1 pound (455 g) small green or savoy cabbage, shredded

1 medium carrot, shredded

2 cups (560 g) Baechu Kimchi (page 102), finely chopped and strained

1 pound (455 g) garlic chives, chopped

1 bunch scallions, thinly sliced

3 cups (450 g) cooked sweet potato noodles

1 block (1 pound/ 455 g) firm tofu, drained and crumbled

¼ cup (60 ml) sesame oil

¼ cup (30 g) cornstarch

2 packages (16 ounces/ 455g each) Shanghai-style dumpling wrappers

Dumpling Dipping Sauce (page 268)

1   In a skillet, heat 2 teaspoons oil over medium heat. Sauté the onion, garlic, and ginger until the onion is translucent and slightly caramelized. Transfer the mixture to a large bowl and let it cool.

2   Add another 2 teaspoons oil to the skillet and cook the mushrooms with a pinch of salt, stirring occasionally, until the mushrooms release all their liquid and the pan is almost dry. Add them to the bowl with the onions.

3   Add another 2 teaspoons oil to the skillet and cook the cabbage with a pinch of salt, stirring occasionally, until the pan is almost dry. Add the cabbage to the bowl with the onions and mushrooms.

4   Add another 2 teaspoons oil to the skillet and cook the carrot with a pinch of salt, stirring occasionally, until the pan is almost dry. Add the carrot to the bowl with the other vegetables. Set this aside to cool to room temperature.

CONTINUES

5   When the vegetables have cooled, drain off any liquid that has accumulated in the bottom of the bowl, then add the kimchi, chives, scallions, sweet potato noodles, crumbled tofu, sesame oil, cornstarch, and 1 tablespoon salt. Mix everything together well and taste for salt. (This mixture can be prepared up to 3 days in advance and stored in the refrigerator.)

6   When you are ready to make the dumplings, prepare a small dish of water and line several baking sheets with parchment paper. Place about 1 tablespoon filling in each dumpling wrapper. Using your finger, paint a little water around the edge of the wrapper. Fold the wrapper in half and pinch the edges closed, or make it fancier by forming a few pleats. Place each finished dumpling on the baking sheet and repeat until you've used all the filling. Freeze the dumplings directly on the baking sheet until they harden, then pack them into plastic freezer bags, where they will last 3 to 4 months. (They do not refrigerate well.)

7   To cook fresh or frozen dumplings (see Note), heat a nonstick frying pan or well-seasoned cast-iron skillet with just enough canola oil to coat the bottom. Add just enough dumplings so that they are not overcrowded and don't touch. Brown the dumplings on their bottoms, then add about $\frac{1}{4}$ inch (6 mm) of water, cover the skillet, and steam the dumplings until nearly all the water evaporates.

8   Remove the cover and let the dumplings fry again, just long enough to crisp them slightly, then serve them immediately with the dipping sauce.

For Koreans, dessert, or *hu-shik*—which really means "after meal"—used to mainly be seasonal ripe fruit. We'd have Korean yellow melon in July or a really juicy peach in August; watermelons in late summer; grapes or persimmons in fall. You'd just slice them up and eat them out of hand, then in winter you'd have toasted chestnuts, peeled and eaten at the table. Historically, finishing every meal with something very sweet was just not what we did—instead we looked to nature.

Of course, all that's changed—there are now multiple Korean restaurant chains focused only on sweets, where people line up for over-the-top desserts all day long, including shaved ice masterpieces and Korean versions of French pastries seasoned with red bean and green tea.

The desserts in this chapter are not those new fanciful things, but mainly all the sweet things I ate growing up: an elegant sponge cake with jam; a sweet pancake seasoned with nuts and brown sugar; a simple raw-sugar caramel you can make at home. I also snuck in a soju-filled cantaloupe, just for fun.

HU-SHIK
DESSERTS

CASTELLA CAKE

This sponge cake is deliciously light and fluffy, and it goes great with afternoon tea and some marmalade or jam. Castella cake comes to Korea by way of Japan, where the cake was inspired by a similar one made by the Portuguese. My recipe is based on one that my mother used to make for our family. It is not difficult to make, but you do need to pay attention to every detail and not rush the process, which is specifically designed to give the cake lift and airiness. That includes sifting the flour, slowly adding ingredients over time, and baking it at a slightly lower temperature than you'd expect. If you don't have a sifter, shake the flour through a wire mesh strainer or beat it with a wire whisk or a fork. The key is to aerate the flour to give the cake that perfect lift.

```
I like to serve this
with Korean jujube
"tea jelly," which
is essentially jujube
jam, sold jarred in
Korean and Asian
markets. Jujubes, or
daechu, are sweet,
maroon berries that
look a lot like dates—
in fact many people
call them Korean
dates.
```

Makes 1 (5 ½ by 10 ½-inch (14 by 27 cm) loaf

```
Cooking spray

7 large eggs, at
  room temperature

1¼ cups (250 g)
  granulated sugar

¼ cup (60 ml)
  whole milk

¼ cup (60 ml) honey

1½ cups (200 g)
  bread flour,
  sifted

1 teaspoon
  kosher salt
```

1   Preheat the oven to 300°F (150°C). Spray the loaf pan liberally with the cooking spray and then line the bottoms and sides with parchment paper.

2   Using a stand mixer fitted with the beater attachment (or a hand-held mixer or an egg beater), beat the eggs on medium speed until well blended. Turn up to medium-high speed and with the motor running, add the sugar one-third at a time over about 10 minutes. Don't rush this process: It is important to go slowly to ensure airiness.

3   In a small saucepan, combine the milk and honey and heat over very low heat just to lukewarm, stirring constantly until the honey melts, about 15 seconds. If too hot, the milk will curdle.

4   Lower the speed to medium, then add half of the warm milk mixture to the egg mixture and beat it in for just a few seconds. Then add half of the bread flour and the salt, beating at low speed until it is completely incorporated.

5   Add the rest of the warm milk mixture, beating at medium speed until it is well incorporated. Then add the remaining bread flour, and beat until it is well incorporated. (At this point, the batter should be fluffy, and light yellow ribbons should form when you lift up a beater. If your batter is not light and fluffy, you might end up with a dense Castella cake that's more like pound cake than sponge cake, but it will still taste good.)

6   Gently pour the batter into the prepared pan and tap it to get rid of air bubbles. Then bake the cake until a toothpick inserted in the center comes out clean, about 50 minutes to 1 hour.

7   Let the cake cool in the pan for 10 minutes, then invert it onto on a wire rack. Once the cake has cooled completely, slice into thick rectangles and serve. (Cake or leftover slices can be frozen for up to a month, then defrosted. They're best warmed in a toaster oven.)

GOGUMA MATTANG

CANDIED SWEET POTATOES

These caramelized sweet potatoes are a common dessert found in Korean Chinese restaurants, but my mother also used to make it at home in Korea. I add a little salt, because it makes them even better. You want to find butter-fleshed Japanese sweet potatoes with purple skin for this dish, and baby ones, if possible, which are even sweeter.

Serves 4

1 pound (455 g)
  Japanese sweet
  potatoes, peeled

4¼ cups (1 L) plus
  1 tablespoon
  canola oil

¼ cup (50 g)
  granulated sugar

1 teaspoon toasted
  sesame seeds

Kosher salt

1   Cut the sweet potatoes in half lengthwise, then slice them into ½-inch (12 mm) half-moons.

2   In a large saucepot, heat 4¼ cups (1 L) oil to 360F (180C), or until the end of a wooden chopstick sends up bubbles when you place it in the oil, and line a plate with paper towels.

3   Fry the sweet potatoes a few at a time, making sure not to crowd the pot, until they are golden brown, about 7 to 10 minutes. Remove from the oil with a strainer or slotted spoon to the paper towels. When all the sweet potatoes are fried, set them aside.

4   Line a baking sheet with waxed paper.

5   In a small saucepan, combine the sugar and 1 tablespoon oil over medium-high heat. Slowly and constantly swirl the oil over the sugar in the bottom of the pot by lifting and tilting the pan, until the sugar melts and becomes light caramel colored, about 1 to 2 minutes.

6   Remove the pan from the heat and add the sweet potatoes, tossing them quickly until they are covered with the caramel. Remove them to the waxed paper, making sure they are separated, then immediately sprinkle them with the sesame seeds and salt to taste.

7   Let the sweet potatoes cool, then serve warm or at room temperature. These are best the day they are made.

RIPE SUMMER TOMATOES
WITH TOFU CREAM

You can serve this as either an ultra-modern dessert or *banchan*. I have memories of eating tomatoes for dessert on a hot, late summer day when I still lived in Korea. My mother would pick sweet-as-can-be tomatoes from our garden and cut them up, then sprinkle salt and sugar over and we'd eat them like the delicious summer fruits that they are! This is my own version, with some additional complexity and creaminess from a thick sauce made of silken tofu and a drizzle of bright, nutty perilla oil, though sesame oil is also delicious. You can use any tomato, as long as it is very ripe and in season, but I really like Jersey beefsteaks.

Serves 6 to 8

2 pounds (910 g) ripe summer tomatoes

½ pound (225 g) silken tofu

2 cloves garlic

1 tablespoon soy sauce

2 tablespoons rice wine vinegar

1 tablespoon perilla or sesame oil

2 to 3 large perilla or basil leaves

¼ red onion, thinly sliced and soaked in cold water

1 teaspoon granulated sugar, plus more to taste

½ teaspoon kosher salt, plus more to taste

1   Wash and dry the tomatoes. Cut them into large cubes or ½-inch (12 mm) slices.

2   In a blender or a mortar and pestle, combine the tofu, garlic, soy sauce, rice wine vinegar, and oil and process until smooth. Set the tofu cream aside.

3   Thinly slice the perilla leaves and drain the red onion, gently patting it dry.

4   Spoon the tofu cream onto a serving plate and lay the tomato pieces on top.

5   Sprinkle the tomatoes with sugar and salt, adding more of both to taste, and garnish with the perilla leaves and red onions. Serve immediately.

HOTTEOK
BROWN SUGAR FILLED DESSERT PANCAKES

I used to eat these sweet street treats as a small child almost every time I accompanied my grandmother to the market. These yeasted, filled pancakes are hot, pillowy, and have just the right amount of crisp from the oil you cook them in. It's important not to cook them too fast, so that the dough has time to do its yeasty thing and the nutty brown sugar filling has time to melt into a gooey sauce. It's also important not to eat them too fast: That filling is still blazing hot right out of the pan!

Makes about 12 pancakes

1 tablespoon
  instant yeast

2 cups (480 ml) warm
  water

½ cup (110 g)
  packed brown
  sugar

3 tablespoons
  sesame seeds

2 tablespoons
  crushed or finely
  chopped almonds
  or walnuts

2½ cups (315 g)
  all-purpose
  flour, plus extra
  for dusting

2 tablespoons
  granulated sugar

Olive oil

2 teaspoons kosher
  salt

1 In a small mixing bowl, combine the yeast and warm water. Stir it vigorously and let it sit for 5 minutes in a warm place.

2 In another small mixing bowl, combine the brown sugar, sesame seeds, and nuts and set aside.

3 In a large bowl, combine the flour, sugar, 2 teaspoons oil, and salt, then add the yeast mixture. Stir with a wooden spoon until the mixture comes together. Turn it out onto a clean, floured work surface and knead the dough until it is smooth, then form it into a ball and place it back in the bowl.

4 Cover the bowl loosely with a clean kitchen towel and let the dough rise in a warm spot for about 1 hour, or until it has doubled in size.

5 Knead the dough on your floured work surface until it is smooth, then form it into a ball, cover it, and let it rise again for about 30 minutes.

6 Divide the dough into 10 pieces and form each into a flattened ball. Poke an indentation into the middle of each ball and fill it with 1 tablespoon of the brown sugar mix. Close up the outer edges of the ball and pinch it shut.

7 In a nonstick pan, heat 1 tablespoon oil over medium heat. When the oil is hot, place one ball of dough in the middle of the pan. When the bottom is browned, flip it over and press it down gently with a spatula until it is a flat pancake about 3 to 4 inches (7.5 to 10 cm) wide. Let it cook until the entire bottom is brown, then flip it over and cook until the other side is fully brown. (It's okay if some of the filling oozes out.)

8 Remove the hotteok to a serving platter and let it cool for about 5 minutes before serving, as the filling is very hot.

9 Repeat steps 7 and 8 with the remaining dough. You can freeze any leftover pancakes, tightly wrapped, and reheat them in a toaster oven.

PPOPGI

RAW SUGAR CANDY

When I was around eight years old, I used to make this rustic candy on spoons and ladles over the flame of a stovetop so often that I would get yelled at for ruining silverware. It was so worth it! I don't know who gave me the idea to melt sugar and add baking soda, but I'm glad someone did: It was my first foray into candy-making. You can make fun designs if you want, or stick toothpicks into the candy circles while they're still warm to make little lollipops. Or you can make a whole sheet of *ppopgi*, let it cool, then break it up into funky bite-size pieces or smaller crumbles to use on ice cream or any other dessert.

Makes about 12 lollipops

1 cup (200 g)
  turbinado or
  "raw" sugar
½ teaspoon baking
  soda

1   In a small, heavy-bottomed pan, melt the sugar over medium heat. Use a wet wooden spoon to stir the sugar, ensuring it melts evenly into a golden caramel color.

2   When the sugar has melted, add the baking soda: The mixture will bubble up and change color rapidly, but continue stirring with the wooden spoon until it is incorporated into the melted sugar and the color turns light brown.

3   To form the candy, lay out a nonstick baking sheet or a sheet of parchment paper or aluminum foil. Drop a little bit of molten sugar on the sheet and pressing it with a nonstick spatula to form a circle, adding a toothpick to make a lollipop. You can also try dropping it to form funky shapes, or spread it out evenly with the spatula, then break it up into large shards, bite-size pieces, or crumbles once it cools.

4   Let the candy cool completely before serving it. It will keep in an airtight container for about a week.

SAMSAEK KYUNG-DAN

SWEET RICE DUMPLINGS IN THREE COLORS

These are both a special occasion thing and an everyday thing: They're made and consumed by all Koreans for holidays and birthdays, especially for little kids, but they're also eaten for breakfast and as a snack. These chewy, sweet dumplings look difficult to make, but they are in fact ridiculously easy—basically water, salt, sugar, and flour made from glutinous or "sweet" rice. (Thanks to the gluten-free movement, this is now easily found.) The three-color toppings—I call them magic dusts, but they're essentially sugar flavored with toasted ground sesame seeds, roasted soybean powder, and sweet red beans—are also fairly easy, though you will have to prep the beans a couple of days in advance. You could just make one of the toppings if you were in a hurry, but a platter of *kyung-dan* (rice cake balls) in three colors (*samsaek*) is really impressive. Plus, leftover toppings are great on ice cream or yogurt.

You almost always see kyung-dan for sale at shops that specialize in *tteokbokki* (page 262). They are sometimes coated in seeds or nuts, or filled with sesame seeds and sugar, or made by special order with various flavors and additions. In the fall there's also *songpyeon*, a special sweet nut-stuffed kyung-dan made for the annual Korean Thanksgiving/harvest fest (*Chusok*) that you form by hand into half-moons. You can eat kyung-dan as a savory meal, too. In fact, you can easily turn this recipe into a savory one by toasting the toasted boiled rice cake balls in a pan with a bit of butter, as you would with gnocchi.

Makes about 40 dumplings

FOR THE RED BEAN TOPPING

- 1 cup (185 g) canned and drained or dried red or adzuki beans
- 2 tablespoons granulated sugar

FOR THE SESAME SEED TOPPING

- ¾ cup (85 g) black sesame seeds
- 2 tablespoons granulated sugar
- ¼ teaspoon kosher salt

FOR THE SOYBEAN POWDER TOPPING

- ¾ cup (75 g) Soybean Powder (page 157)
- 2 tablespoons granulated sugar
- ¼ teaspoon kosher salt

FOR THE DUMPLINGS

- 2 cups (320 g) glutinous (sweet) rice flour
- 2 tablespoons granulated sugar
- 1 teaspoon kosher salt
- 1 cup (240 ml) boiling water

1 Two days before you want to make the dumplings, make the red bean topping: If using canned beans, rinse well under running water. If using dried beans, soak in 3 cups (720 ml) cold water for about 1 hour, then bring the beans and the water to a boil in a medium saucepan, reduce the heat, and let simmer until the water has evaporated and the beans are just tender, 35 to 45 minutes.

2 Drain off any extra water from the beans and place them in a single layer in a large pie pan. Let them dry out, uncovered, in the refrigerator for 2 days, then grind them in a coffee grinder or food processor. In a bowl, mix the ground beans with the sugar and set aside. This can be made up to 2 days ahead and stored in an airtight container.

3 Make the sesame seed topping: Grind the sesame seeds in a coffee grinder or small food processor with the sugar and salt. Transfer to a bowl and set aside. This can be made up to 2 days ahead and stored in an airtight container.

4 Make the soybean powder topping: In a bowl, combine the soybean powder, the sugar, and the salt. This can be made up to 2 days ahead and stored in an airtight container.

CONTINUES

5 Make the dumplings: In a mixing bowl, combine the sweet rice powder, sugar, and salt. Add the boiling water and mix with a wooden spoon.

6 Once the dough comes together, knead it by hand in the bowl just until smooth. Cover the bowl with plastic wrap (or put it in a plastic bag) and set it aside to rest for about 30 minutes.

7 Meanwhile, bring a large pot of water to a boil over medium-high heat.

8 Once the dough has rested, flour a clean work surface. Pinch off pieces of the dough and roll them into 1-inch (2.5 cm) balls, setting them aside on a clean work surface. (You can dust your hands with rice or regular flour if the dough sticks to your hands.)

9 When all the dumplings have been formed, boil them in 2 or 3 batches, letting them cook until they float, about 3 to 4 minutes. Once they rise to the surface, let them cook for few seconds longer, then remove them with a slotted spoon or wire mesh strainer, shaking off excess water, to a nonstick baking sheet or baking sheet lined with parchment paper.

10 When the dumplings have cooled enough to handle, roll one-third of them in the black sesame topping, one-third of them in the soybean powder topping, and one-third of them in the red bean topping.

11 Serve while still warm or at room temperature the day they are made.

HOW-TO

1 Combine the dry ingredients.

2 Add the water and stir until it just comes together.

3 Knead the dough with your hands until it becomes very smooth.

4 Form the dough into a ball and let it sit, covered, at room temperature for 30 minutes.

CONTINUES

5 Pinch off pieces of the dough and roll them into 1-inch (2.5 cm) balls. Dust your hands with rice or regular flour if the dough sticks to your hands.

6 Cook them in the boiling water until they float, about 3 to 4 minutes.

7 Remove them with a slotted spoon or wire mesh strainer to a nonstick baking sheet or baking sheet lined with parchment paper.

8 When the dumplings have cooled enough that you can handle them, roll one-third of them in the black sesame topping, one-third of them in the soybean powder topping, and one-third of them in the red bean topping.

SOJU CANTALOUPE

If you frequent hip Korean food and drink establishments with lots of young people, chances are you've seen a soju watermelon: a blend of soju, fruit, and ice served in a hollowed-out watermelon as a punch bowl. It's light, refreshing, and fun—and it goes down a little too easily. This is the same concept, but made with a delicious summer-ripe cantaloupe.

NOTE: The ubiquitous Chamisul brand of soju is fine, but try to find the Tokki brand, if possible. Brandon Hill of Van Brunt Stillhouse in Brooklyn makes soju just for Insa based on traditional methods he learned in Korea, and it's the best soju I've ever had!

Serves 4

1 ripe cantaloupe
  (3 to 4 pounds/
  1.4 to 1.8 kg)

1 (375 ml) bottle
  soju (see Note)

Kosher salt

3 to 4 cups (720
  to 960 ml/about
  1 tray) ice cubes

1   Cut off the top third of the cantaloupe. Use a large spoon or ice cream scoop to hollow out the shell, reserving the flesh and discarding the seeds.

2   Set the cantaloupe shell aside and puree the flesh of the cantaloupe in a blender until it is smooth. Strain it through a fine-mesh sieve into a bowl or pitcher, pushing down on the pulp to press all the juice through the sieve into the bowl. Spoon out any excess foam that has formed on top of the juice.

3   Add the soju to the juice with a pinch of salt, stirring to mix.

4   Pour the juice into the hollowed-out cantaloupe and gently add the ice, stirring until the liquid is well chilled. Serve immediately with a small ladle, letting each person serve themselves from the cantaloupe.

SHIKHYE

SWEET RICE DRINK

This traditional fermented dessert drink, pronounced "SHIK-hay," is served after a big meal to cleanse your palate and serve as a digestive aid to help your stomach makes sense of all that you just ate for dinner. There are many canned versions of *shikhye* at Korean markets, but as always, homemade is best, and that way you can adjust the sweetness as you like. Like many fermented things, it takes patience, but is otherwise easy to make. I prefer this chilled, often over a few ice cubes.

NOTE: Barley malt powder, sometimes called malted barley powder, is available at Korean markets in the dried grains section and at some health food stores.

Makes about 12 cups

½ pound (225 g) barley malt powder (see Note)

2 cups (280 g) freshly cooked short-grain rice

⅓ to ½ cup (75 to 100 g) granulated sugar, plus more to taste

Toasted pine nuts, for garnish

1   Put the barley malt powder in a large container or nonreactive pot and whisk it thoroughly with 12 cups (2.8 L) water. Let the mixture sit undisturbed for at least 2 hours and up to 5, until all the barley matter has sunk to the bottom. (The longer you let it sit, the clearer your finished shikhye will be).

2   Put the cooked rice in an electric rice cooker or oven-safe pot. If using the oven, preheat the oven to 130°F (54°C). Pour as much of the liquid into the cooked rice as you can while making sure not to get any of the settled barley matter at the bottom into the rice.

3   Close the rice cooker and set it on the "keep warm" setting, letting it sit for 5 hours, or put the pot in the oven for 5 hours.

4   After 5 hours, check to see if any of the grains of rice are floating. (This means fermentation is happening.) If not, let the pot sit at warm/cook for another hour and check again.

5   When the grains have started to float, strain out all the rice into a colander set into a bowl, and pour the liquid out into a clean pot and set it on the stovetop.

6   Rinse the strained rice in cold running water. Add the rice to a clean mason jar, cover it with cold water, and refrigerate the jar until you are ready to serve the drink.

7   Add the sugar to the reserved liquid in the pot, stirring it once or twice, then bring it to a boil over medium-high heat. Let it boil for 4 to 5 minutes, skimming off the scum that rises to the top. Taste the liquid for sugar, adding more to taste as needed. Let the liquid cool, then store it in an air-tight container in the refrigerator.

8   Serve the drink at room temperature, chilled or over ice, adding a few spoonfuls of cooked rice to each glass and garnishing with toasted pine nuts. This will last about a week in the refrigerator.

INDEX

DEDICATION

This book is dedicated to my siblings:
Soojin Kim, Jean Kim Sears, and Kyunghun Kim
Thank you for your crazy love over the years

And to the incredible woman who made us who we are today,
Our grandmother Hyun Keum Sun

ACKNOWLEDGMENTS

To my amazing children, Jasper and Oliver, thanks for always making me laugh and smile!

To my husband, partner, and baby daddy, Benjamin Schneider, I offer my eternal love and gratitude for always being my rock ... even when I am hangry.

To Rachel Wharton, a deep and hearty thank you for our collaboration and our friendship. You make this whole experience super-duper fun! ¡Otra vez!

To Burcu Avsar and Zach DeSart, amazing friends and neighbors who didn't flinch when I said a photo for every recipe! Thank you for creating the most amazing photos.

To Michael Stokes, the genius chef at Insa, for your over-the-top, precise, and delicious recipes such as the better-than-Spam Spam, Soondae, and so much more. Thank you for lending me your measuring spoons.

To Rigo Vazquez, thank you always for your encouragement and your support. Thank you for lending me your measuring cups.

To Yong Sup Shin, thank you for your enthusiasm, partnership, and hard work, and for making me feel really, really old sometimes.

To Jamie Seet, thank you in advance for the idea and execution of Soju Ice Luge. You rock in so many ways!

To Kara Lewis, thank you for taking such great care of the Good Fork and allowing me to write this book without losing my mind. You are one dedicated chef and I am lucky to have you at the helm!

To Jenni Ferrari-Adler, thank you always for Represent'N!

To Hannah Kirshner, Marie Peak, Sunny Lee, and other friends who cook and recook these recipes. Thank you for your help on photo shoot days.

To Ruby Knives and Jessie Lazar, thank you for making beautiful knives and ceramics that I use every day.

To ALL of my coworkers at the Good Fork and Insa, thank you for your support and dedication!

To everyone at Abrams who really have mastered the Art of making beautiful Books! Especially Holly Dolce, editor with the most, and Deb Wood, truly an amazing designer, thank you for your vision and encouragement!

Last but not least, to all of my friends and family who have encouraged me along the way—Gam Sa Ham Ni Da! (Thank you with a deepest bow—the ninety-degree kind that makes other people bow back.)

Editor: Holly Dolce
Designers: Deb Wood and Heesang Lee
Production Manager: Rebecca Westall

Library of Congress Control Number:
2017956844

ISBN: 978-1-4197-3240-9
eISBN: 978-1-68335-325-6

Printed and bound in China
10 9 8 7 6 5 4 3 2 1

Abrams books are available at special
discounts when purchased in quantity
for premiums and promotions as well
as fundraising or educational use.
Special editions can also be created
to specification. For details, contact
specialsales@abramsbooks.com or the
address below.

ABRAMS The Art of Books
195 Broadway, New York, NY 10007
abramsbooks.com